SWEET VIDALIA Onions

BLUE RIBBON RECIPES

This is a collection of **Blue Ribbon Recipes** and other good recipes that include the **Sweet Vidalia Onions.**

BLUE RIBBON RECIPES

collected by

Evelyn Rogers
P. O. Box 736
Vidalia, Georgia 30474

2

If Unable to Obtain
"Sweet Vidalia Onions"
Blue Ribbon Recipes
Through your Local Dealer
For information write to
Evelyn Rogers
P.O. Box 736
Vidalia, Georgia 30474

Cover and Illustrations by
Janet Merritt Myers
Jean Greer
Lewis Herndon

BOOK II

ISBN No. 0-9614318-3-0

Library of Congress Catalog Number 86-090484

Printed by
Howell Printing Company
Aiken, South Carolina

ONION-PRODUCING AREA IN THE COASTAL PLAINS
OF GEORGIA
MAY, 1986

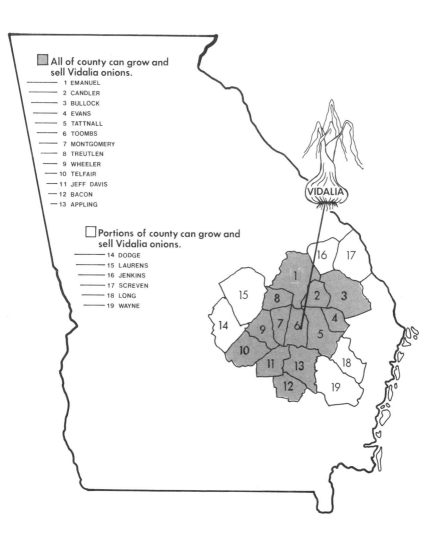

All of county can grow and sell Vidalia onions.
- 1 EMANUEL
- 2 CANDLER
- 3 BULLOCK
- 4 EVANS
- 5 TATTNALL
- 6 TOOMBS
- 7 MONTGOMERY
- 8 TREUTLEN
- 9 WHEELER
- 10 TELFAIR
- 11 JEFF DAVIS
- 12 BACON
- 13 APPLING

Portions of county can grow and sell Vidalia onions.
- 14 DODGE
- 15 LAURENS
- 16 JENKINS
- 17 SCREVEN
- 18 LONG
- 19 WAYNE

VIDALIA

SWEET VIDALIA ONION
"The Onion You Can Peel Without Crying!"

The sweetest onion ever eaten! It is the Vidalia onion! It gets its name from a small town in southeast Georgia, north of the Great Attamaha River that flows to the Atlantic Ocean near Savannah, Georgia.

About forty years ago, the Vidalia State Farmers' Market sold sweet onions. It was the central point for onion growers and buyers. When orders were made they were referred to as "Vidalia onions."

The "Vidalia Onion Variety" means all existing yellow Hybrid Granex varieties. When combined with the South Georgia soil and climate of the area it matures into what has become a gourmet's favorite.

The seeds are planted the first of September then harvest begins about the first of May. It takes eight months for the sweet onion to mature. Other onions take 90 to 120 days to mature.

The harvesting is done by hand labor. Onions are graded and packed in three sizes; small, medium and jumbo. They are available fresh from the fields May through July. However, with the use of conditioned air storage facilities, they will be available until December. If you buy onions in large quantities and use some of the methods that are suggested in this book you can use them from your freezer when the fresh ones are gone.

NEW VIDALIA ONION LAW

Georgia has a new law that sets limits on the production area of Vidalia onions. The law requires registration of producers, packers, and sellers, and it includes a felony violation for packaging, labeling, or selling imposter onions as Vidalias. The law allows production of Vidalia onions within 13 counties and in parts of 6 other counties, all within the heart of the traditional Vidalia onion-growing area.

Also other Georgia onion growers outside of the designated areas may apply to the Georgia Department of Agriculture for permission to grow and sell onions, under a Vidalia label.

Before purchasing Vidalia onions, consumers should read bag labels carefully. This label illustrates the information required by law to be on each bag of Vidalia onions sold.

The label below is one sample of several types of tags used by growers and distributors in the production area of the Sweet Onion.

HURRAY! HURRAY! VIDALIA ONIONS AVAILABLE AT CHRISTMAS!

You can purchase Vidalia onions in most stores at Christmas. Because of the high moisture content in the Vidalia onions it is necessary to store them in conditioned/air storage facilites from three to six months. This prolongs the shelf life of the onions. As soon as you buy onions refrigerate them immediately!

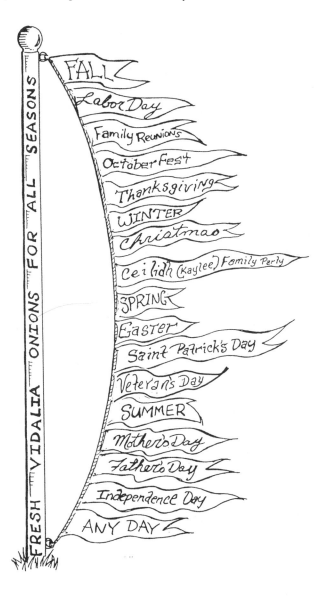

VIDALIA ONION BLOSSOMS

1. Select firm onions 3 to 4 inches wide.

2. Cut ½ inch off the top of onions ONLY. Peel the outside skin to root end with your fingers. DO NOT CUT THE
ROOT END. Rinse in cold water.

3. Use an apple corer to cut the onion into 8 sections. Place
a rubber band around the onion and use a sharp knife to
cut another 8 sections. From the top of the onion cut out
1 inch of the center without cutting the root end.

4. Place the onion blossom into a bowl of hot water for
5 to 10 minutes. Remove and drain.

5. Put the blossom in a bag of *Seasoned flour; gently cover
the petals.

   *Seasoned flour:
      1 cup all-purpose flour
      1 teaspoon paprika and 1 teaspoon garlic salt
      ½ teaspoon salt and ½ teaspoon cayenne
   Sift dry ingredients together and keep in plastic bag.

6. Prepare the deep-fry pot. It should have enough cooking
oil to cover the onion. (About 2 quarts in large deep-fry pot.)

7. Place the floured onion into the *Batter. Use a teaspoon
to separate the petals and insert batter evenly.

8. *Batter: (For 3 medium onions or 2 jumbo onions.)
      1 cup complete buttermilk pancake mix
      ¾ cup water
      1 teaspoon paprika and 1 teaspoon garlic salt
      1 teaspoon all-purpose seasoning

   Mix dry ingredients; add water and mix thoroughly. Stir
the batter well. (Keep it stirred while dipping the onions.)

-continued on page 7-

VIDALIA ONIONS BLOSSOMS cont'd

9.   Place the onion into the deep-fry basket, then into the deep-fry pot. Cook at 375 degrees F. for 4 to 8 minutes or until light brown. Remove the fried onion from the basket with a large slotted spoon or skimmer. The center should be well-cooked. Check it. Drain on a doubled, thick paper towel.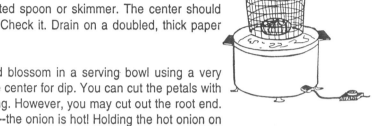

10. Put the fried blossom in a serving bowl using a very small bowl in the center for dip. You can cut the petals with a knife for dipping. However, you may cut out the root end. **BE PREPARED**--the onion is hot! Holding the hot onion on it's side with the paper towel, cut out the root end with kitchen scissors or knife.

11. Select a bowl that will hold the petals in place. Slide the hot onion into the bowl using the paper towels. Insert a small bowl in the center of petals for your favorite dip or *Honey Mustard dip.

> Mix ¼ cup of spicey brown mustard and
> 1 Tablespoon honey.

PS   Start with three onions. The first onion is a trial test, the second one should turn out good, the third one will be perfect! (Well almost perfect.)

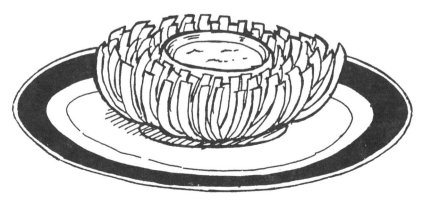

VIDALIA ONION SUNFLOWER

1. Select a large onion. Cut off the top. Peel the onion skin to the root with your fingers. Cut the petals using an apple corer with 8 sections. Put rubber band around onion and cut another 8 sections. Trim out the center, about 1 inch.

2. Use 1 ounce of yellow food color to 2 cups hot water. Soak the onion petals for 40 minutes in the bowl of hot water. Remove, drain and dry with paper towels.

3. Place the yellow onion in a bag of *Seasoned Flour, recipe page 6. Gently cover the petals.

4. Mix the *Batter, recipe page 6, and add ¼ ounce of yellow food color. Put cut floured onion in bowl of batter and cover petals using a teaspoon to separate them.

5. Place onion into a deep-fry basket then into deep-fry pot that has enough cooking oil to cover the onion. Cook at 375 degrees F. for 4 to 8 minutes. Drain on thick paper towels. Be sure the center of onion is well done.

6. Select bowl that will hold petals together. Hold the onion in the thick paper towels, cut out the root end with kitchen scissors. Place fried onion around sides of bowl with cocktail cup in the center for-*"Brown Honey Mustard Dip".
   *Brown Honey Mustard Dip:
      ¼ cup spicy brown mustard
      1 Tablespoon honey
      1 Tablespoon dark brown barbeque sauce
         Spinach leaves for garnish

VIDALIA ONION "ROSE"
"A beautiful decorative centerpiece"

1 onion, 3 inches wide
Apple corer, red food color, hot water

1. Select a uniform size onion. Cut the top but not the root end. Peel outside onion skin to the root with your fingers. Rinse.

2. Use the round apple corer with 8 sections. Sharpen the cutting edges. Place the onion on a cutting board, press the corer down to the root end leaving ¾-inch uncut.

3. Mix one half ounce food color in two cups of hot water. Put the cut onion in the red, hot water for 40 minutes. Check for desired color.

4. Remove the onion from the hot water with a large spoon. Use a bowl to turn it over to keep the petals together and drain. Place in the center of a fancy plate and arrange green parsley around the "rose." Refrigerate until it is needed for your table.

5. Experiment and try all the food colors.

PS--This will be a decorative conversation piece you have made with your clever hands.

BLUE RIBBON RECIPES

THANKSGIVING TURKEY DRESSING

4 cups cooked cornbread
2 cups biscuit
1 cup chopped Vidalia onion
¼ cup chopped green onion
½ cup chopped celery
1 teaspoon sage
1 egg, beaten
3 cups broth
1 teaspoon sugar
2 Tablespoons vegetable oil
    Salt and pepper to taste

In a saucepan add a half cup of water, onions and celery. Boil until tender. Cut cornbread and biscuit into small pieces in a large mixing bowl. Pour in broth; add remaining ingredients. Stir until the bread has absorbed the broth. Put the cooked onions and celery in mixture and stir until it is completely mixed.

In a well-greased baking pan, pour the mixture. Bake in hot oven at 350 degrees F. for 40 minutes or until dressing is brown.

VIDALIA ONION CHRISTMAS AMBROSIA

1 cup chopped Vidalia onion
4 oranges, peeled and cut into sections
1 orange sliced for garnish
½ teaspoon dry mustard
¼ cup sherry wine
¼ cup salad oil
½ teaspoon salt
1 Tablespoon sugar
½ cup white raisins
¼ cup grated coconut

In mixing bowl, combine mustard, wine, oil, salt and sugar. Stir in chopped onion and chill for 1 hour. Before serving add orange sections, raisins and coconut. Garnish with orange slices and onion rings if desired. (You must use white raisins to get the right taste.)

    Waste not an onion!
Refrigerate them as soon as possible.

SWEET VIDALIA ONION CAKE
"Best in the World"

2 cups all-purpose flour
2 teaspoons baking powder
1 teaspoon salt
4 Tablespoons butter
2½ cups chopped Vidalia onions
1½ cups granulated sugar
½ stick butter
⅓ cup shortening
3 eggs
1 cup milk

Heat oven to 350 degrees F. Grease and flour two 9-inch pans. Sift together flour, baking powder and salt in large mixing bowl.

In heavy skillet, melt 4 Tablespoons butter, saute' onions until tender. Pour in mixing bowl to cool.

Cream sugar with softened butter and shortening. Beat until fluffy. Add eggs, beat slowly. Then add flour mixture and milk. Beat for 3 minutes. Add sauteed onions. Stir thoroughly. Pour into pans. Bake about 30 minutes or until wooden pick inserted comes out clean. Cool in pans for 10 minutes; turn out on wire rack and cool completely. Frost with *Creamed Icing.

*Creamed Icing:
  1 stick butter
  1 package cream cheese (8 ounces)
  1 box powdered sugar
  1 cup finely chopped pecans (optional)
Cream butter and cream cheese. Add sifted sugar, beat one minute and stir in pecans. Frost cake.

ONION CASSEROLE

3 pounds Vidalia onions, sliced
1 pound grated sharp cheese
  Salt and pepper to taste
1 bottle ketchup (14 ounces)

Peel and slice onions about ¼ inch thick. Boil until tender and drain. Grate cheese. Layer in casserole dish starting with onions, then cheese, salt and pepper and cover with ketchup. Make into two layers. Bake in hot oven, 375 degrees F. for 20 minutes or until cheese has melted.   Anita N. Estroff

ONION PICKLES

4 quarts small Vidalia onions
⅓ cup salt
4 cups sugar
1½ teaspoons tumeric
1½ teaspoons celery seed
2 Tablespoons mustard seed
½ teaspoon ground allspice
2 teaspoons prepared horseradish (optional)
3 cups distilled 5% acidity vinegar

Method: Prepare onions (Whole - 1½ to 2 inches diameter.) Sprinkle with salt and cover with ice and let stand at least 3 hours. Drain well. Mix other ingredients in stainless steel or enamel pot, add onions and heat to boil but do not boil. Pack in sterlized jars and seal. Yield. 6-8 pints. (Depending on size of onions).
Annie C. Z. Bruner

SALMON STEW WITH VIDALIA SWEET ONIONS

1 can salmon (1 pound)
½ cup chopped Vidalia onion
  Salt and pepper to taste
1 Tablespoon corn oil
2 cups cooked long grain rice

In saucepan cook salmon, onion, salt, pepper and corn oil for 10 minutes. Pour over hot steamed rice. Serves 6. Rubye Jean Bland

"O-DEER"

2 jumbo Vidalia onions
1½ pounds ground venison
Oil
2 small green onions, chopped
¼ pound Mozzarella cheese, grated
2 medium banana peppers, chopped
  Salt and pepper to taste
¼ teaspoon chili powder
2 Tablespoons Worchester sauce
12 strips of red rind hoop cheese, 3 inches long

Boil jumbo onions until soft enough to separate and make onion shells. Brown the venison in a skillet in oil; combine the venison and remaining ingredients (except hoop cheese).
Stuff onion shells with venison mixture. Bake at 350 degrees F. for 30 minutes. Top each stuffed onion shell with 2 slices of cheese and place in oven until cheese melts. Remove and serve. James Castleman

SWEET ONION SAUSAGE CASSEROLE

5 Vidalia onions, sliced
12 Ritz crackers, crushed
1 pound sausage meat, browned in skillet and drained
1 can cream of mushroom soup
½ teaspoon salt
¼ teaspoon seasoning salt
½ cup Cheddar cheese, grated
1 small jar pimento pepper

Put onions in bottom of 12 x 7 inch dish, next put crackers and add sausage meat. Add a layer of onions; add cream of mushroom soup, salt and seasoning salt. Next add layer of cheese and pimento. Bake in preheated oven at 350 degrees F. for 40 minutes.   Wayne Dasher

VIDALIA ONION CHILI RELISH

2 gallons tomatoes
2 teaspoons each of cloves, allspice, cinnamon, celery seed, mustard
    seed
Dash of ginger
8 jumbo Vidalia onions
8 bell peppers
4 hot peppers
1 quart vinegar
4 Tablespoons salt
6 cups sugar

Scald and peel tomatoes. Tie ALL spices in cloth bag. Chop onions and peppers. Put all the ingredients together in an enamel pot. Simmer for 15 minutes, then boil for 1 minute. Put into jars and seal them. Makes about 14 pints.
                                                Mary Frances Hall

SWEET AND SOUR ONIONS
"A zesty addition to any meal!"

4 large sweet Vidalia onions
¼ cup boiling water
¼ cup cider vinegar
¼ cup melted margarine
¼ cup sugar

Peel and slice onions. Arrange in baking dish. Mix remaining ingredients and pour over the onions. Bake for 1 hour in 300 degrees F. oven.

When purchasing Vidalia onions be sure the peeling is dry and tight, not flakey.

VIDALIA ONION WITH CHEESE SAUCE

12 medium Vidalia onions
1 teaspoon salt
4 Tablespoons butter
4 Tablespoons flour
2 cups milk
1 cup grated cheese
½ teaspoon Worcestershire sauce
2 hard-boiled eggs, grated
　Paprika and parsley to taste

Peel and wash onions; cook in boiling, salted water until tender. Drain and cool. Place onions in serving dish. Set aside.

In top of double boiler, blend butter and flour until smooth; add milk gradually, stirring constantly. Add cheese and Worcestershire sauce, cover tightly and keep over hot water until ready to use. Pour over onions. Garnish with grated eggs, parsley and paprika. It is ready to serve.　　　　　　Mary Frances Hall

BAKED VIDALIA ONIONS IN SHERRY CREAM SAUCE

3 cups sliced, pre-cooked Vidalia onions, drained
⅓ cup sherry
1 cup light cream
½ teaspoon salt
¼ teaspoon pepper
2 Tablespoons pimento
1 small jar mushrooms, sliced
3 Tablespoons butter
¼ cup grated sharp Cheddar cheese

Arrange drained onions in shallow baking dish. Combine sherry, cream, salt, pepper, pimento and mushrooms. Pour over onions, dot with butter. Sprinkle with cheese, cover and bake at 350 degrees F. for 20 minutes. You may substitute sour cream for light cream, if desired.　　　　　　Bessie J. Harrelson

OVEN FRIED GROUPER

2 pounds grouper fillets or other fish fillets
　Salt to taste
1 cup milk
1 cup bread crumbs
4 Tablespoons butter

Cut fillets into serving-size portions. Add the salt to the milk, dip fish in milk and roll in crumbs; place in well greased baking pan. Pour melted butter over fish. Place pan on shelf near top of a very hot oven about 400 degrees F. and bake 10 minutes or until fish flakes easily when tested with a fork. Serve immediately or on hot platter with hot Vidalia Onion Rings, page 25.

POTATO AND VIDALIA ONION CASSEROLE

2 pounds lean ground beef, browned and drained
4 Tablespoons oil
6 large white potatoes
6 large Vidalia onions, medium sliced
2 cans cream of mushroom soup
  Salt and pepper to taste

Season meat and brown in oil. Peel and thinly slice potatoes. In large baking dish, make alternate layers of potatoes, onions and meat; season each layer. Pour soup on top and bake at 350 degrees F. for 45 minutes.

Connie Grimes

VIDALIA ONION CORNMEAL DUMPLINGS

1 bunch of mustard greens, cleaned, washed and stems removed
  Water
  Salt to taste
  Vegetable oil

Cut mustard into small pieces before putting them into a large pot and cover with water. Add salt and oil. Boil for 20 to 30 minutes over medium heat until greens are tender. Take out the mustard greens and use the stock for dumplings.

Dumplings:
  1½ cups plain meal
  ¾ cup self-rising flour
  1 teaspoon sugar
  1 egg beaten
  ½ cup chopped Vidalia onion
  Water

Mix dry ingredients well. Stir in egg, onion and add enough water to make a stiff dough. Drop by rounded tablespoons into boiling stock, and cook slowly for about 15 minutes. Serve with pork roast or with the mustard greens.

TOMATO AND VIDALIA ONION PIE

1 9-inch deep dish pie crust
3 large tomatoes, sliced
8 slices bacon, fried crisp
1 medium onion, chopped
1½ cups sharp cheese, grated
1 cup mayonnaise

Bake frozen pie crust about 8 minutes in 300 degree F. oven.
Line bottom of pie crust with sliced tomatoes. Top with crumbled bacon and onion. Mix cheese and 1 cup mayonnaise (add more if needed). Spread over tomatoes. Bake at 350 degrees F. for 30 minutes.

VIDALIA ONION JAM

6 medium onions, sliced
4 Tablespoons butter
2 teaspoons vegetable oil
½ teaspoon salt
⅓ cup brown sugar

In heavy skillet, melt butter and vegetable oil. Add onions and saute' until they are slightly brown, about 8 minutes. Season with salt. Reduce heat, stirring constantly until caramel color and tender. Stir in brown sugar until dissolved. Put in jars and refrigerate until ready to serve. May be heated again. Serve with chicken or turkey.

ELEGANT BAKED FISH WITH VIDALIA ONIONS AND LEMON GARNISH

1 large baking fish of your choice, 3 to 5 pound bass, red snapper
1 cup minced celery
½ cup water
6 Tablespoons butter or margarine
1 large, tart cooking apple, minced or grated
4 cups day-old bread, cubed
1 teaspoon dried sage (optional)
¾ teaspoon salt
½ teaspoon lemon pepper
½ cup minced Vidalia onion
12 small sweet onions, 1½ -inch diameter
 Nutmeg (optional)

In small saucepan, melt butter in water with celery. In large mixing bowl, combine all other ingredients, except onion and pour the butter mixture over them. When mixed the ingredients should be loose but moist enough to handle easily.

The backbone of fish should be removed to allow for stuffing. Stuff fish loosely with mixture and place on a prepared baking dish. Brush with butter. Do not lace. Bake uncovered at 450 degrees F. for 10 minutes. Reduce heat to 350 degrees F. and bake for 45 minutes to one hour or until golden brown and flaky.

While fish is baking remove husk from onions, wash and place in buttered glass baking dish. Dot with butter and sprinkle with salt and nutmeg. Bake uncovered about 20 minutes or until tender.

When fish is ready, remove to large heated platter and garnish with baked onions, lemon wedges and seedless grapes. Serves 8. Fish can be prepared early in the day for use later.

Doris Pearson

 Remember to store your Vidalia onions in the refrigerator as soon as possible after purchasing them.

OLD FASHIONED BRUNSWICK STEW

1 fresh, cleaned, medium complete hog head
1 fresh hog jowl

Boil the head and jowl until the meat falls off the bones. Pour off the water, so that the stew will not be greasy. Clean the pot and use fresh water. (Use and iron kettle if you have one.)

5 pounds sweet onions, chopped
½ cup butter
5 pounds potatoes, diced
4 cans tomatoes (1 pound each)
8 ounces vinegar
Crushed red pepper, black pepper and salt
3 lemons, juice and rind (take rind out before stew is cooked)
2 cans white creamed corn (only white creamed corn will do)
1 bottle of catsup (16 ounces)

Cook the onions in butter until tender. "You might think they will get done before you add the potatoes, but they won't." Add the potatoes to the onions and cook. Stir in cut-up meat. "Don't grind the meat, cut it up."
Include with the meat the cut-up tongue and ears. Stir constantly; it burns easily and will ruin the stew. Add tomatoes, crushed red pepper, black pepper, salt, vinegar, lemon juice, rind and catsup. Lastly, add canned white creamed corn. Watch carefully and cook slowly, stirring all the time. Cook it until it has reached a consistency when it will not run off a spoon.
"It takes a long time to cook good stew."   Nora Davis Moreland

VIDALIA ONION-SAUERKRAUT SALAD

1 large Vidalia onion, chopped
1 large can sauerkraut, drained (27 ounces)
1 green pepper, chopped
1 cup chopped celery
1 small jar pimento. drained
1 cup vinegar
1½ cups sugar

Peel, wash and chop onion, soak in ice water for 30 minutes. In large salad bowl mix sauerkraut, green pepper, celery, pimento and onion, drain. In small bowl dissolve sugar in vinegar. Pour over all the ingredients, mix well. Chill for 2 hours before serving. Serve with chicken, turkey or pork.   Helen Butler

**If you have a Vidalia onion to sprout,
put it in a saucer and place it on the window sill to grow.
Cut off some of the green sprouts when needed for a recipe.**

PIT BARBECUED PORK
Georgia State Grand Barbecue Coooking Champion, 1986

Sauce:
- 3 bottles catsup (10 ounces each)
- 1 small bottle Lea and Perrins Worcestershire sauce (8 ounces)
- 4 ounces vinegar
- Crushed red pepper, black pepper
- Salt to taste
- 1 teaspoon peanut butter

Mix: bring to a boil and let simmer, stirring well. If too much vinegar, add more catsup. Peanut butter makes it smoother.

15 to 17 pound fresh pork ham or 12 to 14 pound fresh pork shoulder

Rub the meat good with salt on both sides before cooking. Do not put anything on it while cooking. It takes from 10 to 12 hours to cook a pork shoulder or ham. Spareribs take less time.

Serve with Barbecue Sauce. George D. Moreland

STUFFED VIDALIA ONION CASSEROLE

- 6 medium Vidalia onions
- 1 teaspoon cooking oil
- ½ pound mushrooms, sliced
- ½ cup chopped celery
- ½ cup rice, cooked in chicken broth
- 3 cups chopped boiled chicken
- 1 can cream of mushroom soup
- Salt and pepper to taste
- ¼ cup water

Peel and wash onions. Core centers. Reserve enough of onion centers, using 1 cup, to saute' in cooking oil with mushrooms and celery. Cook rice in chicken broth.

In large mixing bowl, add chicken, cooked rice, salt and pepper. Mix in onions, celery and mushrooms. Stuff cored onions with mixture and put in baking dish. Place remaining stuffing mixture over and around onions. Combine soup with ¼ cup of water. Pour soup and water over onions and stuffing. Bake in preheated 350 degree F. oven until soup is bubbly. Onions should remain crunchy. Charlotte K. Grimes

Baked Onions to Store

Peel onions, leave whole. Place in casserole dish. Pour melted butter over onions. Shake all-purpose seasoning on top of each one. Bake in 300 degree F. oven for 25 to 30 minutes. (Do not overcook). Cool onions and place in freezer bags. Use onions as needed. Doris Pearson

NINE BEAN SOUP MIXTURE
"Very Filling"

Mixture
>1 pound pearled barley
>1 pound black beans
>1 pound dried red beans
>1 pound pinto beans
>1 pound navy beans
>1 pound great northern beans
>1 pound lentils
>1 pound split green peas
>1 pound black-eyed peas

Combine all of the ingredients mix well. Divide mixture into 10 two-cup packages for individual cookings.

Recipe:
>2 cups Nine Bean Soup Mixture
>2 quarts cold water
>1 pound ham, diced
>1 large Vidalia onion, chopped
>1 clove garlic, minced
>½ teaspoon salt
>1 can tomatoes, undrained and chopped (16 ounces)
>1 can tomatoes with green chilies (10 ounces)

Sort beans and wash. Put in Dutch oven, cover with water at least 2 inches above beans. Soak and parboil for 5 minutes, drain. Add 2 quarts of water with the next 4 ingredients. Cover, bring to a boil, reduce heat, simmer for 1½ hours or until beans are tender. Add remaining ingredients and simmer for 30 minutes. Yields 8 cups. Serve with *Thin Cornbread.

*Thin Cornbread:
>1 cup corn meal
>½ cup self-rising flour
>1 Tablespoon sugar
>1 egg, beaten
>1 cup milk
>½ stick butter, melted

Mix together all the ingredients. Pour into greased baking pan in order that cornbread will be 1-inch thick. Bake 25 minutes in 425 degree F. oven, Drizzle butter on top..   Dot Eames

Vidalia Onion Sandwich
Slice an onion (any thickness), use bread and butter pickles, mayonnaise and bread. One sandwich is delicious! One more, just plain good!

SWEET ONION BUTTERED HOT ROLLS
"You will eat them before you get to the table"

1 loaf frozen "Bake at Home" bread dough
*Sweet Onion Butter

Place frozen loaf on greased baking pan to thaw and rise at room temperature. Cover with wax paper. Let dough rise at room temperature to half of the volume, about 2½ hours. Cut dough with sharp knife in pieces of 1½-inch diameter. Roll pieces of dough in balls.

Roll the ball of dough around once in melted *Sweet Onion Butter mixture. Place on baking sheet about 2 inches apart. Cover with wax paper. Let rolls rise until double in size, about 2 hours.

Preheat oven to 375 degrees F. Place rolls in oven and bake for 25 minutes or until golden brown.

***Sweet Onion Butter**
    ½ cup butter, melted
    ¼ cup finely grated Vidalia onion
    ½ teaspoon garlic powder
    2 sprigs parsley, minced (optional)

Mix ingredients, stir well. Mixture will keep for days in the refrigerator.
Betty J. Pope

TURKEY HAM ROLL-UPS

    5 cups chopped cabbage, cooked and drained
    ½ cup shredded Swiss cheese
    8 thin slices fully cooked turkey ham (about 1 pound)
    ¼ cup chopped Vidalia onion
    2 Tablespoons butter or margarine
    3 Tablespoons flour
    1½ cups milk
    2 teaspoons horseradish mustard
    ½ cup shredded Swiss cheese
    1 Tablespoon chopped parsley
    1 Tablespoon butter or margarine, melted
    ¼ cup bread crumbs

Combine cooked cabbage and ½ cup of cheese; spoon about 3 tablespoons onto each ham piece and roll-up. Place, seam side down, in a baking dish.

Saute' onions in 2 tablespoons butter or margarine; blend in flour. Add milk and mustard and gently bring to a boil, stirring constantly. Add ½ cup cheese and parsley. Pour over turkey ham rolls. Combine 1 tablespoon melted butter and bread crumbs and sprinkle over cheese sauce. Bake uncovered at 375 degrees F. for 25-30 minutes.

VIDALIA ONION TART

Filling:
    2 pounds Vidalia onions
    2 egg yolks
    6 Tablespoons heavy cream
    ½ cup water
    ¼ pound bacon - cut in strips
    1 teaspoon flour
    1 teaspoon salt
    ¼ cup peanut oil
    Pie Pastry (see recipe below)

Slice onions thinly and layer in large saucepan. Add 1 teaspoon of salt to them and set aside to draw out the water for at least 30 minutes. Add ¼ cup of oil and ½ cup water. Steam onions until transparent and water is cooked out. Meanwhile, place sliced bacon in a small amount of water in a shallow pan and blanch to remove excess fat. Bacon should be limp. Pour off liquid and coarsely chop. When water is cooked out of onions, add 1 teaspoon of flour and stir to dissolve.
    Remove from heat and add 2 egg yolks and cream with the onions. Stir constantly.

Pie Pastry:
    2 cups all-purpose flour
    ½ cup unsalted butter
    2 egg yolks
    1 teaspoon salt
    5½ -6 Tablespoons cold water

Sift flour onto a pastry board, cloth or dough bowl and make a large well in the center. Pound butter to soften slightly or have at room temperature. Place butter, egg yolks, salt and smaller amount of water in the well and work together with the fingertips of one hand until partly mixed. Gradually work in flour, pulling dough into large crumbs using the fingertips of both hands. If the crumbs are dry, sprinkle over a tablespoon or more water. Press dough firmly together - it should be soft, but not sticky. Work on a lightly floured board, pushing dough away with the heel of the hand and gathering it up with a dough scraper until smooth and pliable. Press dough into a ball. Wrap in foil or plastic wrap and chill for 30 minutes.
    It can be stored tightly wrapped in the refrigerator for up to 3 days.

Directions:

Roll pastry to about ½ " thickness in a rectangular shape. Place pastry on an oiled baking sheet. Crimp edges of pastry if desired. Beat an egg yolk with a pinch of salt and brush over the entire pastry. This is called "egg glazing" and helps the filling adhere to the pastry. Pierce pastry with a fork in several places to prevent bubbles from forming while baking.
    Spread onion mixture over the pastry and sprinkle the chopped bacon on top.
    Bake at 300 degrees F. for 10 to 15 minutes or until nicely browned. Cut into 1" squares for hors d'oeuvres. May be made a day ahead and reheated. Wait to cut until after heating if made ahead.
    May be baked in individual tartlet pans or a pie plate.

Put cut, left over onions in plastic bag and freeze for casseroles.

VIDALIA ONION PIE

2 pounds onions, thinly sliced
1 stick butter
3 eggs, well beaten
1 cup sour cream
¼ teaspoon salt
½ teaspoon white pepper
¼ teaspoon Tabasco sauce
2 9-inch pastry shells
Grated Parmesan cheese

Bake pie shells at 350 degrees F. for 8 minutes. Saute' onions in butter. Combine eggs, sour cream and seasonings. Add to sauteed onions. Pour mixture in pastry shells. Top with Parmesan cheese. Bake at 350 degrees F. for 20 minutes, then at 325 degrees F. for 15 minutes or until slightly brown.

PARSLEY AND SWEET ONION BUTTER

½ cup butter
1 Tablespoon lemon juice
1 Tablespoon chopped parsley
2 Tablespoons grated Vidalia onion
Salt and pepper

When you grate the sweet onion, the water content is so high there will be lots of juice, use it.

Cream butter as for a cake, add lemon juice a little at a time and when well blended stir in chopped parsley (that has been washed), grated onion, salt and pepper. Form into a ball or flat cake and chill thoroughly before serving or melt butter mixture and pour over vegetables.

To Prepare parsley:

Wash and dry thoroughly; remove all stalks. Chop fine; place the chopped parsley in the corner of a cloth and twist the cloth so that none may escape. Hold under the water faucet and press the parsley with thumb and finger to get rid of all excess green coloring. Otherwise the sauce may be dull, instead of creamy with particles of green parsley distributed through it.

RICE PILAF

¼ cup chopped sweet Vidalia onion
¼ cup chopped celery
¼ cup chopped green pepper
2 Tablespoons margarine
1 cup chicken broth
½ cup sliced mushrooms
⅓ cup uncooked rice

Combine onion, celery, green pepper, and margarine in 1-quart saucepan. Saute' on medium heat for 3 minutes or until tender. Stir in remaining ingredients; cover. Reduce heat; cook for 20 minutes or until liquid is absorbed.

STUFFED VIDALIA ONIONS

6 large Vidalia onions
1½ cups cornbread, crumbled
½ cup cooked potatoes, diced
1 cup broth (or water)
1 hard boiled egg
1 envelope instant cream of chicken soup mix
  Salt and pepper to taste
  Paprika

Peel and wash onions. Simmer in enough water to cover onions for about 10 minutes or until almost tender. Remove pulp from onions with apple corer, leaving only the two outside layers of the onions. Add onion pulp to other ingredients. Place ingredients in blender and blend for a few seconds for a smooth stuffing. Place onion shells in lightly greased muffin tins or custard cups. Fill with stuffing and sprinkle with paprika. Bake in slow oven 325 degrees F. for about 30 minutes. To serve, place stuffed onions around main dish.   Effie Purvis

VIDALIA ONION CUSTARD

2 Tablespoons melted butter
3 cups chopped Vidalia onion
¾ cup light cream
2 eggs, beaten
½ teaspoon salt
  Dash pepper
  Bread crumbs

In skillet, melt butter, put in onions and ¼ cup cream; slowly cook until onion is tender. Fill 6 greased custard cups ¼ full with hot mixture. In bowl, beat eggs, remaining cream, salt and pepper together until light. Fill cups ½ full with egg mixture. Sprinkle with bread crumbs.

Place cups in a pan of hot water. Bake at 350 degrees F. for 25 to 30 minutes until set. Serve immediately.

APPLE-ONION PIE
**"The onion you can eat like an apple!
The apple you can eat like an onion!"**

3 large sweet delicious apples, peeled, cored and sliced
2 large Vidalia onions, peeled and thinly sliced
1 cup chicken broth (1 chicken bouillon cube, 1 cup water)
1 cup Graham cracker crumbs
3 Tablespoons butter

Peel, core and slice apples into ¼-inch slices. Peel and thinly slice onions. Layer the onion slices in a buttered 9½-inch pyrex pie plate. Put a layer of apples on onion slices, another layer of onions, ending with apples. Pour one cup broth over the layers, then sprinkle cracker crumbs on top. Drizzle melted butter over the crumbs. Bake in oven at 350 degrees F. for 30 minutes or until top has browned. "It is delicious!"

Store Vidalia onions in the refrigerator as soon as you purchase them.

SHE-CRAB SOUP

8 ounces crabmeat, fresh or frozen
3 quarts milk
¼ pound butter
1 small Vidalia onion, finely chopped
¼ cup crab roe or yolks of 3 hard-cooked eggs, grated
1 teaspoon paprika
¾ cup all-purpose flour
   Salt and pepper to taste
¼ cup sherry wine

Thaw crabmeat if frozen. Drain. Remove any remaining shell or cartilage. Flake the crabmeat.

Heat milk until hot, but not boiling. In the top of a double boiler, melt butter; add onion and let simmer for 3 minutes. Add crab meat and crab roe or grated egg yolk. Stir. Add paprika and stir. Fold in flour and simmer for 5 minutes. Pour milk into the double boiler and stir until blended; add salt and pepper. Keep on low heat for 30 minutes. Add sherry to each serving.

SHE-CRAB SOUP WITH VIDALIAS

3 Tablespoons butter
1 medium Vidalia onion, chopped
2 teaspoons flour
1 quart whole milk
2 pounds flaked white crab meat
¼ pound crab roe OR 2 eggs yolks of hard cooked eggs
   Pepper and mace to taste
1 pint cream
½ cup sherry

In a heavy skillet, melt 1 tablespoon butter and saute' onions. In top of double boiler, melt 2 tablespoons of butter and blend in flour. Stir in onion, add 1 quart of milk, stirring constantly. Add crab meat and roe. Stir. Add seasonings and cook for 20 minutes. Add the cream and stir well. Remove from heat and add sherry. Garnish with minced parsley.

CAVIAR SWEET ONION DIP

4 Tablespoons black or red caviar
1 Tablespoon catsup
½ cup mayonnaise
½ cup sour cream
2 Tablespoons grated Vidalia onion
2 teaspoons lemon juice

Mix all of the ingredients together. Use as dip with unsalted crackers or use as dressing for fish salads.

Hold an onion under water while peeling, it will keep the eyes from watering.

SAVANNAH CRAB STEW

1 Tablespoon butter
2 Tablespoons grated sweet Vidalia onion
1 Tablespoon flour
1 quart milk
1 teaspoon salt
    White pepper to taste
1 Tablespoon Worcestershire sauce
    Dash of Tabasco
1 Tablespoon lemon juice
½ pound crab meat
¼ cup sherry

In heavy saucepan, melt butter, saute' onions, blend in flour gradually stir in milk. Stir until smooth. Add seasonings. Remove from heat. Stir in lemon juice, crab meat and sherry. Heat through.

VIDALIA FRIED ONION RINGS

1 cup buckwheat flour or all-purpose flour
2 Tablespoons corn meal
1 cup beer
½ teaspoon salt
2 jumbo Vidalia onions
4 cups oil

Combine flour, meal, beer and salt in mixing bowl stirring fast and thoroughly. Let sit about 3 hours at room temperature. Peel, wash, and slice onions, separate into rings and soak in ice water for 30 minutes. Towel dry. Heat oil in deep fry pot. Dip each ring separately into batter. Drop into hot oil. Fry in oil until brown. Onion rings may be placed in baking dish and kept in oven at 200 degrees F. until ready to serve.

VIDALIA ONION RINGS

2 large sweet onions
2 egg yolks
1½ cups buttermilk
1½ Tablespoons vegetable oil
1¼ cups flour
1 teaspoon salt
1¼ teaspoons baking powder
2 egg whites

Peel and slice onions into ½ -inch slices. Separate into rings. Beat egg yolks; add buttermilk, oil and sifted dry ingredients. Beat egg whites until stiff; fold into buttermilk mixture. Dip oinion rings into batter. In deep hot oil in a large saucepan fry rings, a few at a time until golden brown. Drain on paper towels.

ONION-APPLE 'N BEER

⅓ cup butter or margarine
8 small sweet Vidalia onions, quartered
1 cup beer
½ cup maple syrup
3 apples, cored, do not peel, cut in ¼ inch slices

In skillet melt butter; saute' onions about 15 minutes but do not brown. Pour in beer; syrup and apples. Cook uncovered about 15 minutes or until most of liquid has evaporated, stirring occasionally. Serve with sliced turkey.

SCALLOPED POTATOES WITH SWEET VIDALIA ONIONS
"Great for Covered Dish Dinners"

4 medium potatoes, cooked, peeled and sliced
2 medium Vidalia onions, thinly sliced
1 cup buttermilk
1 cup sour cream
1 Tablespoon dried parsley
  Salt and pepper to taste
  Bread crumbs
1 cup grated Cheddar cheese

Place potatoes in pot, cover with water, cook untill tender. Cool potatoes, peel and slice. Place 1 layer in buttered casserole dish. Place layer of onion. Mix buttermilk, sour cream and seasonings. Pour over layers. Place another layer of potatoes, then onions. Pour remaining milk mixture over layers. Sprinkle bread crumbs over top of casserole. Bake for 20 minutes in 350 degrees F. oven. Remove from oven, sprinkle grated cheese on top of bread crumbs. Return to oven and cook for 10 minutes or until cheese melts.

OGEECHEE CATFISH STEW

1½ pounds streak-a-lean pork meat, sliced
3 pounds white potatoes, sliced
3 pounds Vidalia onions, sliced thin
2 pounds steamed and deboned catfish, 2 X 3-inch chunks
  Salt and pepper to taste
¼ cup water

Fry streak-a-lean, drain, and break into small pieces. (Save drippings to pour over stew). Pour small amount of fat drippings in bottom of large dutch oven. Place layer of potatoes, layer of catfish and layer of onions. Sprinkle crumbled pork on top of layer. Salt and pepper and repeat layers until pot is filled. Pour water then bacon drippings over the top. Simmer covered over low heat for 2 to 3 hours. This taste great when camping at the Ogeechee River!

VIDALIA ONION FISH STEW

4 cups water
2 teaspoons white wine
1 each of Vidalia onion, parsley sprig, carrot
    Salt and pepper to taste
    Dash of vinegar
3 pounds bass, sole or whitefish filleted
3 egg yolks
2 cups Garlic Sauce (recipe below)
6 slices of toasted French bread

Put liquids, onion, parsley, seasonings, vinegar and carrot in kettle and bring to a boil. Cook for 10 minutes. Add fish to boiling broth and poach for 5 to 10 minutes or until fish flakes easily, and not over cooked. Remove fish to a hot platter and strain broth. Cook down to about 2 cups. Beat egg yolks in top of double boiler. Gradually add hot broth, then set pan over hot water, not boiling, cook and stir until thickened. Gradually stir in 1 cup of *Garlic Sauce (recipe below) and blend until mixture is creamy and heated thoroughly. Warm six soup plates and place a piece of toast in each. Top with cooked fish and pour some of sauce over all.

*Garlic Sauce:
    4 garlic cloves
    ¼ cup mayonnaise
    1 Tablespoon fresh lemon juice
    1¾ cups mayonnaise

Put garlic cloves in blender, add ¼ cup mayonnaise and lemon juice. Blend well. Add 1 ¾ cups mayonnaise. Mix well.

VIDALIA ONION SOUP

2 medium Vidalia onions, sliced
2 Tablespoons butter
2 teaspoons sugar
5 cups beef broth
    Salt and pepper
5 slices whole wheat bread (toasted)

Melt butter; saute' onions until tender. Stir in sugar and beef broth and heat. Add seasonings. Simmer for 30 minutes over low heat. Put bread in bottom of soup cups; pour soup over bread, or *Whole Wheat Croutons may be used on top of soup.

*Whole Wheat Croutons:
Slice 6 slices whole wheat bread in ½ -inch cubes. Bake in 250 degree F. oven about 30 minutes until dry. For seasoned croutons; use 1 beaten egg white, 1 tablespoon Italian herb seasoning with 1 teaspoon seasoned salt. Beat egg white. Mix seasonings in paper bag. Put bread cubes in egg white, then shake in paper bag with seasonings. Place on baking sheet and bake about 40 minutes in 300 degree F. oven.

CHICKEN PECAN QUICHE

Crust:

    1 cup all-purpose flour
    1 cup sharp Cheddar cheese, shredded
    ½ teaspoon salt
    ¼ teaspoon paprika
    6 Tablespoons oil

Mix dry ingredients and stir in oil. Set aside one fourth of mixture for topping. Place remainder in bottom of 9-inch pie pan. Press with fingers to form a crust. Bake at 350 degrees F. for 10 minutes. Remove from oven.

Filling:

    3 eggs, beaten
    1 cup sour cream
    ¼ cup mayonnaise
    ½ cup chicken broth
    2 cups cooked chicken, diced
    ½ cup sharp Cheddar cheese, shredded
    ¼ cup grated sweet Vidalia onion
    ¼ teaspoon dill weed
    3 drops hot pepper sauce
    ¼ cup pecan halves

Blend first four ingredients, stir in the remaining ingredients except pecans and pour into prepared crust. Sprinkle reserved crumb mixture on top. Garnish with pecan halves. Bake at 325 degrees F. for 45 minutes.

Claire R. Allen

SAUTEED GROUPER
"Catch of the Day"

    2 pounds grouper, fresh or frozen
    3 Tablespoons butter
    2 medium Vidalia onions, sliced
    1 green pepper, seeded and sliced
      Meal
      Seasoned salt
      Pepper to taste

Thaw fish if frozen. In heavy skillet, melt butter, saute' onion and green pepper rings until tender, but not brown. Place in serving dish. Save butter.

Dredge fish lightly in meal; season. Place in skillet; saute'. Cook until fish flakes when pierced with a fork.

Place fish on dish with onions and green peppers. Delicious.

"You Will Want to Catch More"

REFRIGERATE THOSE VIDALIA ONIONS!

SWEET VIDALIA ONION SCALLOP

3 medium onions, sliced
¼ cup butter or margarine
¼ cup chopped green pepper
2 Tablespoons chopped pimento
1 cup grated Swiss cheese
1 cup cracker crumbs
2 eggs, well beaten
¾ cup light cream
   Salt and pepper to taste
2 Tablespoons margarine, melted

In heavy skillet, saute' in margarine the onions and green peppers until tender. Stir in pimento. Place half of onion mixture in shallow baking dish. Sprinkle with half of grated cheese and half of cracker crumbs. Repeat layers of onion and cheese. Beat eggs with light cream, salt and pepper. Pour over onions. Sprinkle top with cracker crumbs, lightly drizzle melted margarine over top. Bake in moderate oven at 350 degrees F. for 25 minutes.

STUFFED VIDALIA ONIONS
(Microwave)

4 small Vidalia onions
1 Tablespoon butter
¼ teaspoon salt
1/8 teaspoon pepper
1 cup herb-seasoned stuffing mix
¼ cup beef broth

Place a piece of plastic wrap large enough to cover stuffed onion in a 1½-quart casserole. Slice onions crosswise into 3 layers. Place bottom slice of onion on plastic wrap in casserole.

Place butter in a 4-cup glass measure. Microwave at HIGH 20 seconds to melt. Stir in salt, pepper, stuffing mix, and beef broth. Place a little of the stuffing mixture on onion slice, put center onion slice on top of stuffing, place a little stuffing on this slice, top with remaining onion slices.

Cover with plastic wrap and microwave on HIGH for 6 to 7 minutes

VIDALIA ONION - CHEESE SUPPER BREAD

½ cup chopped Vidalia onion
1 Tablespoon butter
1 cup Cheddar cheese grated
1½ cup biscuit mix
1 egg, beaten
1 cup milk
1 Tablespoon poppy seed
2 Tablespoons melted butter

Saute' onions in butter until clear. Add half of the cheese to dry biscuit mix. Combine egg and milk, add to the mix. Stir slowly. Add onions. In a greased baking pan spread dough, sprinkle top with remaining cheese and seed. Drizzle melted butter over top. Bake in hot oven about 400 degrees F. for 25 minutes.

GRILLED ONIONS

4 large Vidalia onions
4 Tablespoons butter
4 beef bouillon cubes
Salt and pepper to taste

Remove skins from onions, wash and core. Place 1 tablespoon butter and 1 beef bouillon cube in center of each onion, sprinkle with salt and pepper. Wrap each onion in double thickness of heavy duty foil. Cook on grill about 45 minutes or in oven at 350 degrees F. 45 minutes. To cook in microwave wrap onions in wax paper and cook on high for 20 minutes.

VIDALIA ONION PIE AU GRATIN

Crust:

¼ cup butter
35 saltines

Filling:

2 Tablespoons butter
3 medium Vidalia onions, thinly sliced
½ pound sharp grated Cheddar cheese
1½ cups scalded milk
3 eggs, beaten
Salt and pepper

To make crust: Soften butter and mix with the crushed saltine crackers. Spread in deep dish pie pan, quiche dish or baking pan.

To make filling: Saute' onions in butter in thick skillet. Arrange on cracker crust. Sprinkle grated cheese on top. In a mixing bowl, mix milk, eggs, salt and pepper to taste. Pour over the onions and cheese. Bake at 350 degrees F. oven for 30 minutes.

VIDALIA ONIONS IN CURRY CREAM SAUCE

5 medium Vidalia onions, sliced
½ cup butter
½ cup cooking sherry
3 Tablespoons flour
¼ cup water
½ teaspoon curry powder
Salt to taste
1 cup dry herb stuffing

In heavy skillet, melt half of the butter. Add sliced onions and sherry. Simmer 20 minutes or until onions are tender. Mix flour with water and stir into onion mixture. Cook until thickened. Mix in seasonings. In a saucepan, melt remaining butter and mix with stuffing. Pour onion mixture into greased casserole dish, sprinkle stuffing over onion mixture. Bake in preheated oven at 350 degrees F for 20 minutes or until lightly browned. Serve with baked hen.

HOT CHICKEN PASTA STIR-FRY

1½ cups wheel-shaped pasta or harvest pasta
2 Tablespoons vegetable oil
2 whole chicken breasts, skinned, boned and cut into ½-inch cubes
2 small green peppers, cut into strips
1 medium Vidalia onion, sliced
½ teaspoon ground cumin
½ teaspoon cayenne
1 can whole kernel corn, drained (8 ounces)
½ teaspoon salt
2 cans tomatoes with chilies (10 ounces each)
2 Tablespoons cornstarch
1 cup shredded Cheddar cheese

Cook pasta according to package directions, drain. Heat oil in wok or large skillet over high flame. Add chicken; stir fry until pieces turn white. Add green peppers, onion, cumin and cayenne. Stir-fry 3 minutes. Add additional oil, if necessary. Stir in drained pasta, corn and salt. Cover; cook 2 minutes. Drain tomatoes with chilies, reserving liquid. Add tomatoes with chilies to cooked mixture. Mix 2 tablespoons cornstarch with half of reserved liquid. Add to wok; bring to boil, stirring constantly. Reduce flame; sprinkle cheese on top. Cover; heat 2 minutes, or until cheese melts.

SPANISH CHICKEN WITH VIDALIAS

2 whole chicken breasts, halved and boned
1 can chicken broth and 1 can water
2 Tablespoons butter
1 green pepper, cut into strips
1 large sweet onion, cut into wedges
½ teaspoon garlic powder
½ teaspoon cumin
1 teaspoon seasoned salt
2 ripe tomatoes, chopped
2 Tablespoons granulated sugar
1 package yellow rice mix (7 ounces, prepare as directed)
½ cup chopped ripe olives
½ cup grated Cheddar cheese

Place chicken breast halves in a large skillet. Pour the chicken broth over them, then add a can full of water. Bring the liquid to a boil, reduce heat, simmer for 10 minutes. Turn chicken once. Cool. Cut into chunks. Pour off liquid and melt butter in skillet. Saute' green pepper, onion, garlic powder, cumin and seasoned salt for 2 minutes. Add tomatoes, sugar, chicken; stir. Cover and reduce heat to medium low. Simmer for 5 minutes. Spoon mixture over rice and garnish with olives and cheese.

FESTIVE GREEN VIDALIA ONIONS
"For any celebration"

For St. Patrick's celebration serve sandwiches with green onion slices. Use ¼ ounce of green food color in one cup of hot water. Put sliced onions into the green water for 30 minutes. Remove the slices and refrigerate until ready to serve. (Use the green water to cook a pot of rice!)

SOY BURGERS

2 cups cooked soybeans
1 medium Vidalia onion, chopped
½ cup chopped green pepper
½ cup chopped celery
1 carrot, grated
1 egg, beaten
1 cup cracked wheat
2 Tablespoons cooking oil

Mash the beans and chop the vegetables. Add egg and cracked wheat. Mix well, shape into patties. Fry in oil about 12 minutes on each side, until crisp. Drain on paper towel.

JUICY ROASTED CHICKEN

1 4-5 pound chicken
3 cups water
¼ cup soy sauce
1 Tablespoon sugar
1 medium Vidalia onion, chopped
½ cup cooking sherry
1 teaspoon ginger
1 teaspoon salt

Combine all ingredients except chicken. Bring to a boil. Add whole chicken; cook for 10 minutes. Remove from heat and let stand for 20 minutes. Remove chicken from liquid, place in shallow pan with rack and roast at 375 degrees F. about 40 minutes or until tender. Place on serving platter and garnish. (Chicken broth may be cooled and frozen for use later).

Peel, wash and cut into quarter sections those Vidalia onions.
Put into a blender and chop.
Pour the liquid into individual ice trays and freeze.
Take out the cubes, bag them; and freeze.

VIDALIA ONION AND TATER-TOT CASSEROLE

1½ pounds ground beef
1 large Vidalia onion, chopped
1 Tablespoon Worcestershire sauce
1 rib of celery, diced
2 cups shredded Cheddar cheese
1 can cream of celery soup
1 can cream of mushroom soup
1 bag frozen tater-tots

In a heavy skillet brown beef, drain leaving 2 tablespoons of fat in skillet. Saute' onions until tender. Mix onions and beef. Pour into casserole dish. Sprinkle with Worcestershire sauce, celery and cheese. Mix the celery soup and mushroom soup together and pour over cheese. Cover the soup with tater-tots. Bake at 350 degrees F. for 45 minutes.   Ben McDilda

VIDALIA ONION EGG SPREAD
"It's easy and low in calories"

1½ cups cream style cottage cheese, small curd, well drained
2 teaspoons Worcestershire sauce
½ teaspoon salt
¼ teaspoon dry mustard
¼ teaspoon pepper
  Dash of hot pepper sauce
¼ cup chopped sweet onion
¼ cup finely chopped celery
8 hard-cooked eggs, chopped

If desired, press cottage cheese through sieve. Combine in medium bowl with seasonings, onion and celery, stirring until blended. Stir in eggs. Cover and chill several hours or overnight to blend flavors. Serve in lettuce cup as a dieter's salad or spread in crisp celery stalks.

LEFT-OVER VIDALIA ONIONS

Use 1 Tablespoon butter in skillet, melt and add 1 tablespoon honey; stir in about 1 cup of chopped onions and cook 8 minutes. Store in sterilized jar in the refrigerator!

If your onions are not refrigerated, you must do something to preserve them before spoilage occurs. Freeze them whole or chopped.

ONION PIZZA SANDWICH

1½ pounds Vidalia onion
1 clove garlic, minced
3 Tablespoons salad oil
1 can tomato sauce (8 ounces)¾ teaspoon Italian seasonings
1 teaspoon salt
    Dash of pepper
1 pound of ground beef
    Loaf of French bread
    Margarine or butter
½ cup grated Cheddar cheese

Peel and wash onions. Slice thin. Saute' onion and garlic in heavy skillet in salad oil. Add tomato sauce and seasoning. Simmer 5 minutes. Brown ground beef in another skillet in small amount of oil. Add to onion mixture. Cut French bread in half lengthwise. Spread with butter and toast under broiler. Spread with onion mixture. Sprinkle with Cheddar cheese; broil until cheese is melted. Cut in slices to serve.

BAKED RED SNAPPER WITH SOUR CREAM STUFFING

3 or 4 pounds dressed red snapper or other fish, fresh or frozen
1½ teaspoons salt
    *Sour Cream stuffing
2 Tablespoons oil

Thaw frozen fish. Clean, wash and dry fish. Sprinkle inside and out with salt. Stuff fish loosely. Close opening with small skewers or toothpicks. Place fish in a well-greased baking pan. Brush with oil. Bake in oven, 350 degrees F. for 40 to 50 minutes or until done. Remove skewers.

*Sour Cream Stuffing:
¾ cup chopped celery
½ cup chopped Vidalia onion
¼ cup oil
1 quart dry bread cubes
½ cup sour cream
¼ cup diced peeled lemon
2 Tablespoons grated lemon rind
1 teaspoon paprika
1 teaspoon salt

In skillet cook onion and celery in oil until tender. Combine all ingredients and mix thoroughly. Makes about 1 quart of stuffing.

APPETIZERS

CHEESE PECAN BALL

2 to 3 Tablespoons sweet onion relish
2 Tablespoons Heinz 57 Steak Sauce
1 package cream cheese (8 ounces)
1 teaspoon pepper sauce
Garlic salt to taste
1½ cups chopped pecans

Cream cheese should be at room temperature. Mix all ingredients together and form into a ball and chill. You may reserve ½ cup pecans to roll ball for garnish, or sprinkle paprika on the cheese ball and garnish with olives on toothpicks to make it more attractive.   Teresa Bish

VIDALIA ONION AND TURKEY CRESCENTS

¼ pound Louis Rich fully cooked breast of turkey
2 cans refrigerated crescent roll dough

Filling:
1 package frozen chopped spinach, thawed and squeezed dry
1 cup shredded Swiss cheese (4 ounces)
⅓ cup mayonnaise
2 Tablespoons finely chopped Vidalia onion
Pinch of tarragon

Cut turkey into 1/8 inch slices. Cut each turkey slice into four crosswise pieces; set aside. Unroll crescent roll dough. Cut each triangle in half to form two triangles. Roll up as directed on package to form a "mini" crescent. Place on ungreased baking sheet. Bake in 375 degrees F. oven 5-7 minutes until golden brown. Cool. Slice in half lengthwise

Combine filling ingredients; spread scant tablespoon on bottom of crescent halves. Top with turkey and remaining crescent half. Place sandwiches on baking sheet. Cover loosely with foil. Bake in 400 degree F. oven for 15 minutes. Makes 32 appetizers.

CAVIAR YOGURT DIP

⅔ cup plain yogurt
1 Tablespoon parsley, minced (optional)
2 Tablespoons Vidalia onion, grated with juice
1 teaspoon prepared mustard
1 jar Romanoff Red Lumpfish Caviar (2 ounces)

Combine all ingredients. Serve at once or cover and chill. Just before serving, stir. Very good with unsalted crackers or crisp raw vegetables. Makes about one cup dip.

CAVIAR AND VIDALIA ONION BUTTER

½ cup sweet whipped butter, softened
¼ cup Vidalia onion, finely chopped
    Unsalted crackers or *Toast Points
1 jar Romanoff Red Lumpfish Caviar (2 ounces)

Combine softened whipped butter and onion; stir well. Spread on unsalted crackers or *Toast Points. Lightly spread caviar on butter. Place on serving dish. Garnish with lemon wedges.
    *Toast Points: Use 100 percent whole wheat bread, sliced thin. Trim edges. Cut into triangles. Place on baking sheet; bake in 300 degree F. oven until slightly brown or dry.

CONGEALED SALMON MOUSSE

2 packages unflavored gelatin
½ cup cold water
1 can tomato soup, undiluted
1 cup mayonnaise
1 package cream cheese (8 ounces)
½ cup diced celery
½ cup sliced stuffed olives
½ cup chopped green pepper
½ cup chopped sweet onion
1 cup salmon, flaked, bones removed

Dissolve gelatin in cold water. Heat tomato soup, undiluted. Melt gelatin in hot tomato soup. Put in blender with mayonnaise and cream cheese. Add remaining ingredients, mix well. Pour into well-oiled 5 cup mold.

Save those gourmet delights before they spoil. Dry them in the oven. Clean and chop onions. Spread on cookie sheet, place in the oven at the lowest temperature (100-140 degrees F.) Dry for 12 hours. Cool and store in sterilized jars in the refrigerator.

CLAM FONDUE

1 sweet Vidalia, diced
3 Tablespoons butter
½ green pepper, diced
¼ pound processed Cheddar cheese, cubed
4 Tablespoons catsup
1 Tablespoon Worcestershire sauce
¼ teaspoon red pepper or liquid hot pepper
2 cans minced clams, drained (7 ounces each)
2 Tablespoons sherry

In top of double boiler melt butter. Add onion and green pepper. Saute' until soft. Add process cheese, catsup, Worcestershire sauce and red pepper. Place over hot water until cheese melts. Add clams and sherry. Blend well, heat through. Serve with French bread as dip.

VIDALIA ONIONS AND CUCUMBERS

½ cup yogurt
½ cup sour cream
1 teaspoon dill, minced
  Salt (optional)
  Lemon pepper to taste
1 cup cucumbers, chopped
1 cup onions, chopped

Combine yogurt, sour cream and seasonings. In bowl, combine the yogurt mixture with sliced cucumbers and onions, cover and marinate in the refrigerator for at least 2 hours. Spread on toast.

VIDALIA ONION MEXICAN DIP

1 can condensed bean with bacon soup
¼ cup Vidalia onion, finely chopped
1 cup Cheddar cheese
1 can tomatoes and green chilies (10 ounces)
1 Tablespoon hot chili powder
½ cup peanut butter

Heat all ingredients in top of double boiler. Cook and stir over boiling water until cheese is melted and mixture is blended.

BREADED ONIONS

1 pound small Vidalia onions
1 egg, beaten
1 Tablespoon water
½ teaspoon salt
1 cup buttered bread crumbs

Put onions in boiler and cover with water. Boil until tender. Drain onions. Dip in mixture of egg, water, salt, then in bread crumbs. Bake in 400 degree F. oven for 10 minutes.

GEORGIA CLAM BITES

¼ cup Vidalia onion, chopped
1 Tablespoon butter or margarine
1½ Tablespoons all purpose flour
¼ teaspoon Worcestershire sauce
  Dash of garlic powder
¾ cup clams, minced
1 cup water or clam juice
½ cup Cheddar cheese, shredded
1 Tablespoon Parmesan cheese
16 slices bread, crusts removed
½ cup butter, melted

In heavy skillet, saute' onion in butter. Remove from heat. Stir in flour, Worcestershire sauce and garlic powder. Gradually stir in clams and liquid. Cook over medium heat, stirring until thickened and bubbly. Remove from heat; add cheeses and stir until melted. Cool.

Using a rolling pin, flatten bread. Spread 1½ teaspoons of clam mixture on each slice of bread. Roll up. Slice into thirds and place seam side down on greased cookie sheet. Brush with melted butter Bake at 425 degrees F. for 10 minutes.

CRABMEAT AND CHEESE DIP

2 cans (7 ounces) or 2 packages frozen crabmeat, thawed
8 ounces cottage cheese
2 Tablespoons mayonnaise
2 Tablespoons Vidalia onion, minced
1 Tablespoon mustard
1 Tablespoon lemon juice
½ teaspoon salt
  Parsley
  Lemon slices, twisted

Drain crabmeat. Reserve reddest pieces for garnish; put rest in blender. Mix with cheese, mayonnaise, mustard, lemon juice and salt. Heap onto serving dish, garnish with remainder of crabmeat, parsley, lemon slices. Makes 2 cups.

GREEN ONIONS - CHUTNEY CHEESE MOLD

2 packages cream cheese (8 ounce packages)
3 Tablespoons raisins, chopped
3 Tablespoons sour cream
3 teaspoons curry powder
¾ cup roasted peanuts, chopped
1 small chopped Vidalia onion
½ cup chutney
2 Tablespoons chopped green onion
4 Tablespoons crumbled bacon
½ cup coconut for garnish

Mix all ingredients by hand, except coconut. Form into balls. Refrigerate. Roll in coconut. Serve with bland crackers.

BREADS

HOT PEPPER CHEESE BREAD

3 cups Vidalia onions, grated
3 Tablespoons butter or margarine
¾ cup warm water
2 packages active dry yeast
2 cups milk
3 Tablespoons sugar
¼ cup margarine or butter
1 Tablespoon salt
7 cups unsifted all-purpose flour
3 cups sharp Cheddar cheese, shredded
1 can jalapeno chilies, chopped and drained (4 ounces)

In heavy large skillet, saute' onion in 3 tablespoons of butter until tender; set aside. In large bowl, combine water and yeast stirring until yeast is dissolved. In saucepan, heat milk, sugar, butter and salt to scalding point. Let cool to warm, add to yeast mixture. Add 2 cups flour and onion; beat at low speed until blended. Stir in enough remaining flour to make a stiff dough. Turn out on lightly floured surface; knead until smooth and elastic, 8 to 10 minutes. Place in greased bowl, turning once to grease surface. Cover; let rise until doubled. Punch dough down. Divide dough into thirds. Roll each third into 18 x 12 inch rectangle; sprinkle 1 cup cheese over each rectangle, leaving a 1-inch edge. Sprinkle a third of chilies over the cheese. Roll dough up tightly jelly-roll fashion beginning with the long side. Seal edge. Place on 3 greased baking sheets, seam side down, in spiral or coil shape. Cover and let rise until doubled. Bake in 400 degree F. oven 15 to 20 minutes or until golden brown. Makes 3 loaves.

CORNBREAD "LACE" CAKES

1 cup plain meal
1¼ cups water
½ teaspoon salt
1 cup Vidalia onions, finely chopped
    Vegetable oil

Grease heavy griddle with one teaspoon of oil. Heat griddle over medium high heat. It is hot enough when a drop of water sizzles on it. The batter should be thin for "lace" cakes but a little thicker for heavy cornbread cakes. Drop large spoonfuls of mixture on hot griddle to form small cakes. Cook about 3 minutes on each side or until golden brown. Cakes are great served with vegetables or soup.

BRITTLEBREAD

2½ cups all-purpose flour, unsifted
¼ cup sugar
½ teaspoon salt
½ teaspoon soda
½ cup butter, (no substitute)
5 ounces whipping cream
2 Tablespoons minced Vidalia onion

Blend flour, sugar, salt and soda. With pastry blender, cut butter into flour mixture. Add whipping cream and onion;mix to a soft dough. Flour pastry cloth, pinch off dough size of an egg or larger; roll very thin. Sprinkle with sugar or salt. Bake at 400 degrees F. for 6-8 minutes on ungreased cookie sheet. Turn off the heat and allow to crisp in oven. Serve with *She Crab Soup, page 24.

HUSHPUPPIES

2 cups corn meal
1 Tablespoon baking powder
½ teaspoon sugar
   Salt and pepper to taste
2 eggs, beaten
½ cup finely chopped Vidalia onions
1 cup buttermilk (or more)
   Vegetable oil for deep fryer

Mix all dry ingredients and sift into mixing bowl. Add eggs and chopped onions. Pour small amounts of buttermilk stirring gently. Continue with buttermilk until there are no dry spots and mixture has a smooth consistency. Refrigerate until cold, about 2 hours. Heat oil to 360 degrees in deep fryer. Drop mixture by teaspoonful into the hot oil. A larger size will cook on the outside and not on the inside. Fry until golden brown.

VIDALIA ONION BUTTER

¼ cup finely chopped onion
½ cup softened butter
½ teaspoon dry mustard
½ teaspoon white pepper

Mix ingredients together in blender thoroughly. Spread on hot rolls or biscuits.

"Rainey day" onions.
Before your Vidalia onions spoil, peel, clean and chop them.
Spread them on a cookie sheet and freeze in freezer.
Place in small freezer bags; stack flat in the freezer for
cooking stews and soups.

CORN FRITTERS

1 Tablespoon butter
½ cup chopped Vidalia onion
1½ cups finely cut corn from cob or canned creamed corn
¾ cup self-rising flour
½ teaspoon salt
   Dash pepper
1 egg, beaten
2 Tablespoons milk (if corn is very dry)

In skillet melt butter and saute' onion until tender but not brown.
Cut corn quite fine from cob. Sift together flour, salt and pepper. Add egg, onion and corn. (If necessary add milk.) Drop by spoonfuls on hot well-greased griddle or frying pan and fry until golden brown on both sides. If you use canned corn, add two tablespoons of flour to absorb extra moisture.
Cook like batter cakes or make stiff dough and drop in deep fat and fry like doughnuts. Serve with fried chicken or vegetables.

VIDALIA ONION CORN BREAD

½ cup chopped onion
2 Tablespoons butter or margarine
1 package corn bread mix
½ cup sour cream
½ cup shredded Cheddar cheese

Cook onion in butter till tender and clear. Prepare mix according to package directions. Pour into greased 8 x 8 x 2 inch pan. Sprinkle with cooked onions. Mix sour cream and cheese; spoon over the top. Bake in hot 400 degrees F. oven for 25 minutes or till done. Let stand a few minutes before cutting.

VIDALIA ONION BISCUITS

2 Tablespoons finely chopped onion
2 Tablespoons butter, melted
1 package homestyle refrigerated biscuits

In heavy skillet, melt butter, saute' onion until tender. On an ungreased baking pan, place biscuits, making a hollow in the center. Fill hollows with butter mixture. Bake at 400 degrees F. for 8 minutes or until golden brown.

SPOON BREAD

1 cup chopped Vidalia onion
2 Tablespoons butter
1 cup corn meal, stone ground
2 cups boiling water
½ teaspoon salt
1 Tablespoon minced chives
3 eggs
1 cup milk

Melt butter in skillet and cook onions until tender. Stir corn meal very slowly into 2 cups boiling water, add salt and stir the mush over moderate heat for a minute. Remove the pan from the heat and beat in butter with onions and chives. Add the eggs beaten with 1 cup cold milk and beat again.
Pour the batter into a buttered baking dish and bake at 400 degrees F. for 25 minutes until it is well puffed and a pretty brown. Spoon at once onto plates along side ham or other meat.

 Enjoy Vidalia onions in several colors. *Colorful Vidalia Onions, recipe page 65. Use them in decorations and vegetables.

VIDALIA ONION SHORTCAKE

2 cups all-purpose flour
4 teaspoons baking powder
½ teaspoon salt
4 Tablespoons shortening
½ cup milk
2 Tablespoons butter
2 medium Vidalia onions, sliced
1 egg
½ cup cream

Sift flour, baking powder and salt together. Cut in shortening with pastry blender. Add milk and knead dough as quickly as possible. Flatten in a buttered casserole. In a skillet, quickly, melt butter; add onions and saute' until tender. Cool and spread over dough. Beat eggs, cream and salt and pour over onions. Bake in 400 degree F. oven for 15-20 minutes.

CORN CAKES

1 cup self-rising corn meal
½ teaspoon salt
1 teaspoon sugar
½ small Vidalia onion, finely chopped
  (use juice from onion)
1¼ cups water
  Vegetable oil

Combine corn meal, salt, sugar and onion with water and mix well. Grease heavy griddle with one teaspoon of oil. Heat griddle over medium heat until a drop of water sizzles on it. Place large spoonfuls of mixture on hot griddle to form 6 cakes. Cook about 3 minutes and turn. Cook until golden brown.

PEACHY ONION SAUSAGE BAKE

½ pound ground pork sausage, browned and drained
½ cup chopped Vidalia onion
1½ cups buttermilk or complete pancake mix
¾ cup milk
2 Tablespoons cooking oil
1 egg
2 cups sliced peaches, chopped (16 ounce can)

Cook sausage in skillet, remove sausage and saute' onion; drain.

In large bowl combine pancake mix, milk, oil and egg. Stir in onion, sausage and peaches. Pour batter into greased 8-inch pan or baking dish. Bake at 350 degrees F for 40 minutes. Serve with your favorite syrup.

When you get home with that large bag of onions, put them on cardboard in a cool area of the house. Loosen the top of the bag, spread them out so they will get circulating air. REFRIGERATE them as soon as possible.

 # CASSEROLES

SEA ISLAND CRAB CASSEROLE

1 Tablespoon butter
½ cup chopped Vidalia onion
1 pound crabmeat
¼ cup mayonnaise
  Juice of 1 lemon
  Salt and white pepper to taste
3 slices of lemon

In skillet, melt butter; saute' onion until tender. In casserole dish mix onion with crabmeat. Handle lightly, do not pack crabmeat. Spread with mayonnaise. Sprinkle with lemon juice, salt and white pepper. Top with three thin slices of lemon. Cover tightly and bake in 350 degrees F. oven for 15 to 20 minutes.

SQUASH-CARROT CASSEROLE

2 dozen round buttery crackers
1 package cream cheese, softened (8 ounces)
2 cans cream of chicken soup, undiluted
2 eggs, beaten
½ cup butter or margarine, melted
2½ pounds yellow squash, cooked
6 small carrots, grated
1 cup finely chopped sweet Vidalia onion
1 cup herb-seasoned stuffing mix

Place crackers in a greased 13 x 9 x 2 inch baking dish; set aside. Combine cream cheese, soup, eggs and butter; beat well. Stir in squash, carrot, and onion. Spoon into prepared baking dish, sprinkle with stuffing mix. Bake at 350 degrees F in oven for 30 minutes.

Refrigerate Vidalia onions.
Wrap them in paper towels or tin foil, but be sure to refrigerate them. Check them once a week and remove any that are beginning to spoil.

BROCCOLI RICE CASSEROLE

1 small Vidalia onion, chopped
2 Tablespoons butter or margarine
1 can cream of mushroom soup
1 can milk
2 cups fresh broccoli, cooked
¼ pound Velveeta cheese
1 cup rice, cooked

Saute' onion in butter or margarine; add soup, milk, broccoli and cheese; cook until cheese melts. Mix with rice, pour into casserole dish. Bake at 350 degrees F. for 30 minutes.

CHICKEN AND ONION CASSEROLE

¾ cup Vidalia onion, chopped
¾ cup celery, chopped
4 Tablespoons peanut oil
1 chicken, boiled and boned
1 package broccoli frozen, cooked and drained (10 ounces)
1 small can mushrooms, drained
1 can mushroom soup
1 cup grated Cheddar cheese
¼ cup roasted peanuts, chopped
   or almonds

Saute' onion and celery in peanut oil in heavy skillet. Add rest of ingredients and blend well. Reserve some peanuts for the top. Cook in 2-quart casserole at 350 degrees F. for 30 minutes.

BROILED CHICKEN CASSEROLE

8 chicken breasts
   Salt and pepper to taste
2 cups water
1 medium Vidalia onion, sliced
1 bell pepper, sliced
1 can chicken broth
6 medium-sized potatoes, quartered
¼ stick margarine, melted

Place chicken breasts in buttered casserole dish. Salt and pepper to taste and add water; cover, cook until tender. Place a slice of onion and bell pepper on each piece of chicken, add chicken broth and potatoes. Cover the dish and cook until potatoes are done; remove cover and brown.

CREOLE EGGPLANT CASSEROLE

1 large eggplant
1 large Vidalia onion, chopped
3 ribs celery, diced
1 Tablespoon Worcestershire sauce
1 small green pepper, diced
2 pimentos, diced
15 saltine crackers, crumbled
2 eggs, beaten
1 can cream of mushroom or chicken soup, undiluted
½ cup grated cheese
  Salt and pepper
  Paprika

Wash, peel and cook eggplant in salted water until tender, drain. Cut into 1" pieces. Combine remaining ingredients except cheese. Pour mixture in large, buttered casserole dish. Sprinkle with grated cheese and paprika. Bake in 350 degree F. oven for 30 minutes.

"HURRY-UP DINNER CASSEROLE WITH SWEET VIDALIA ONIONS"

½ cup chopped Vidalia onion
1 Tablespoon butter
1 can cream of celery soup
½ cup milk
½ cup grated cheese
½ cup cooked diced potatoes
1 cup cooked cut green beans, drained
1 Tablespoon diced pimento
1 can salmon, drained (7¾ ounces)
2 Tablespoon buttered bread crumbs

In skillet, saute' onion in melted butter until tender. Blend in soup, milk and cheese. Heat and stir until cheese melts adding more milk if necessary. Stir in potatoes, green beans and pimento. Use margarine to grease the bottom of a baking dish. Pour a third of potato mixture into it. Break up salmon with a fork and put a layer on top of the mixture. Repeat layers. Sprinkle bread crumbs on top. Bake in medium oven about 20 minutes.

POTATO VIDALIA ONION CASSEROLE

2 pounds frozen hash brown potatoes
1 cup diced onions
1 can cream of chicken soup
16 ounces sour cream
½ cup melted margarine
8 ounces grated sharp cheese
  Salt and pepper

Thaw potatoes about 30 minutes. Mix all ingredients in a large bowl Place in a 9 x 13 inch baking dish. Bake at 350 degrees for 1 hour.

VIDALIA ONION-OKRA-TOMATO BAKE

½ pound bacon
1 medium Vidalia onion, finely chopped
1 package frozen cut okra, thawed (10 ounces)
1 small green pepper, finely chopped
2 Tablespoons precooked rice
1 can tomatoes (16 ounces)
1 Tablespoon sugar
   Dash garlic powder and pepper
¼ teaspoon salt
1 Tablespoon Parmesan cheese
¼ cup dry bread crumbs
1 Tablespoon melted butter

In large heavy skillet, fry bacon until crisp. Drain on paper towel and crumble; set aside. Cook onion and okra in bacon grease left in skillet. Drain and place in greased 1½ -quart casserole. In mixing bowl add green pepper, rice and crumbled bacon; mix well, and stir in tomatoes, sugar, garlic powder, salt and pepper. Pour mixture over okra; top with cheese. Combine bread crumbs and melted butter; sprinkle on top of casserole. Bake at 350 degrees F. about 45 minutes.

CHEDDAR CHEESE-VIDALIA ONION BAKE

6 medium-sized onions, thinly sliced
¼ cup butter
¼ cup all-purpose flour
2 cups milk
2 cups shredded Cheddar cheese
½ teaspoon salt

Place onion in a 2-quart casserole that has been buttered; set aside. Melt butter in a heavy saucepan over low heat; add flour, stirring until smooth. Cook 1 minute, stirring constantly. Gradually add milk; cook over medium heat, stirring until thickened and bubbly. Add cheese and salt, stirring until cheese melts and sauce is smooth. Pour cheese sauce over onion. Bake, uncovered in moderate oven 350 degrees F. for about 45 minutes.

SALMON CASSEROLE
"Dieters delight"

1 large can pink salmon
   Salt and pepper to taste
½ cup chopped Vidalia onion
2 cups cracker crumbs or crushed saltines
4 teaspoons butter, melted
1 can chicken gumbo soup

Butter baking dish. Alternate layers of salmon, seasonings, onion and cracker crumbs in baking dish. Pour butter over top. Cover with soup. Bake in 350 degree F. oven until top is browned. Serve immediately.

EGGPLANT CASSEROLE

1 medium eggplant, cut in ½" cubes
1 cup tomato sauce
½ cup water
1 medium Vidalia onion, diced
1 small green pepper, diced
½ cup diced celery
1 small can mushrooms
    Garlic powder, salt and oregano to taste

Peel and parboil eggplant for 5 minutes or until tender, drain and cut into ½" pieces. Combine other ingredients. Arrange layers in casserole, alternating with eggplant. Bake ½ hour at 350 degrees F.

GOLDEN HAM CASSEROLE WITH VIDALIA ONIONS

2½ cups noodles
1 Tablespoon vinegar or lemon juice
1 cup milk
1½ cups diced cooked ham
2 eggs, beaten
½ teaspoon salt
1/8 teaspoon pepper
1 cup grated cheese
½ cup cooked peas
1 Tablespoon grated Vidalia onion
    Buttered bread crumbs or crushed cereal flakes

Cook noodles in boiling salted water; rinse with warm water. Stir vinegar into milk; let stand for a few minutes. Combine milk, ham, eggs, salt, pepper, cheese and noodles; add peas and onion. Pour into buttered casserole; top with crumbs. Bake in 375 degrees F. oven for 30 minutes. (Chicken or turkey may be used instead of ham.)

CORN CASSEROLE

4 cups cream style corn
1 pound ground beef
1 medium Vidalia onion, chopped
2 eggs, beaten
½ cup milk
1 cup soda cracker crumbs
    Salt and pepper to taste

In skillet lightly brown hamburger meat. Put meat in mixing bowl, reserve some of the fat, saute' onions. Combine all ingredients. Pour into greased casserole dish. Bake at 350 degrees F. for 40 minutes or until top is brown.

SHRIMP-RICE CASSEROLE

2 boxes long grain rice (6 ounces)
¼ cup butter
1 bell pepper, chopped
1 large Vidalia onion, chopped
2 pounds shrimp, cooked and chopped
1 cup sharp cheese, grated
1 Tablespoon lemon juice
1 teaspoon Worcestershire sauce
1 teaspoon dry mustard
½ teaspoon black pepper
2 cans mushroom soup

Cook rice, use package directions. Melt butter in heavy skillet saute' pepper and onion until tender, about 4 minutes.

Mix remaining ingredients, pour into greased baking dish. Bake in moderate oven 350 degrees F. for 40 minutes.

SALMON BAKE SUPREME WITH VIDALIAS

¼ cup butter
¼ cup chopped sweet Vidalia onion
¼ cup all-purpose flour
½ teaspoon thyme leaves
2 cups milk
2 packages frozen cut green beans (9 ounces) or 1 pound fresh
    green beans, cooked and drained
1 can salmon, drained and flaked (1 pound)

In heavy skillet, melt butter; saute' onion until tender, blend in flour and seasonings. Remove from heat; stir in milk. Heat to boiling, stirring constantly. Boil and stir 1 minute. Stir in beans and salmon. Turn into a 1½-quart buttered casserole. Cover and bake in a preheated 400 degree F. oven, 30 minutes or until hot and bubbly.

FRESH GARDEN VEGETABLE CASSEROLE

1 medium Vidalia onion, diced
½ pound carrots, diced
¾ pound squash, sliced
¾ pound zucchini squash, sliced
½ pound cabbage, shredded
3 Tablespoons margarine, melted
1 tomato, diced
¼ pound Cheddar cheese, grated
¼ pound Swiss cheese, grated
2 Tablespoons grated Parmesan cheese
¼ pound roasted peanuts, chopped
2 Tablespoons wheat germ

Saute' onion, carrots, and yellow squash in margarine until tender. Add zucchini and cabbage and cook until all vegetables are tender. Fold in tomato, Cheddar cheese, Swiss cheese and peanuts. Mix thoroughly. Bake in casserole at 350 degrees F. for 10 minutes or until cheeses are melted. Top with Parmesan cheese and wheat germ before serving.

VIDALIA ONION-EGG PIZZA

Crust for 2 pizzas:
      4 cups biscuit mix
      ½ cup cold water
      2 Tablespoons oil
Mixture for 2:
      10 hard-cooked eggs
      1 teaspoon salt
      ½ teaspoon pepper
      2 cans tomatoes, sliced and drained (no.2 cans)
      2 cans tomato paste (6 ounces)
      1 cup finely chopped sweet onion
      ½ teaspoon oregano
      ½ teaspoon thyme
      ½ teaspoon salt
      3 cups Cheddar cheese, shredded

Prepare crust by stirring water into biscuit mix until moistened. Form into 2 balls and place on lightly floured surface; knead 8 minutes. Pat dough out on a cookie sheet or pizza pan into a 12-inch circle. Pinch up edges of dough to make a rim and brush surface with oil. Slice eggs and arrange evenly over dough, reserving 10 center slices for garnish. Sprinkle eggs with salt and pepper.

In bowl, combine tomatoes, tomato paste, onion, salt, oregano, and thyme. Spread mixture over eggs, top with shredded cheese. (Cover with aluminum foil and refrigerate, if you want to cook later.) Bake in a 450 degree F. oven for 20 minutes or until crust is brown and cheese is melted and bubbly. Serve immediately with an egg slice on top of each wedge of pizza.

CHICKEN DINNER CASSEROLE

      1 package frozen broccoli cuts (10 ounces)
      ⅓ cup chopped Vidalia onion
      1 cup grated, Cheddar cheese
      2 eggs, slightly beaten
      ½ cup mayonnaise
      1 can cream of mushroom soup
      1 soup can of water
      ¾ cup converted rice, uncooked
      ½ cup sliced mushrooms
      6 chicken breasts (boneless, if desired)
         Paprika

Cook onions with broccoli according to package directions, drain. Mix together next 7 ingredients. Add broccoli and onion and stir. Pour into a 9 x 13 inch baking dish and place chicken on top. Sprinkle with paprika. Bake at 350 degrees F. for 1 hour.

FRIED RICE CHICKEN CASSEROLE

2 cups cooked, cubed chicken
1 Tablespoon lemon juice
1 can cream of mushroom soup
1 teaspoon salt
½ teaspoon pepper
½ cup mayonnaise
½ cup almond slivers
½ cup water
3 Tablespoons margarine
½ cup chopped Vidalia onion
2 cups rice
   Salt to taste
6 cups water or chicken broth
1 cup crushed potato chips

Combine first 8 ingredients in a large bowl. Set aside. In a large skillet, melt margarine and saute' onion and rice for 5 minutes; add salt and water or chicken broth; cover and simmer for 20 minutes. In a large casserole place half of rice, chicken mixture then remaining rice. Sprinkle with crushed chips. Bake at 350 degrees F. for 30-45 minutes. Serves eight.

KING CRAB AU GRATIN

2 packages frozen King crab (6 ounces)
3 Tablespoons margarine
3 Tablespoons flour
1 cup milk
½ cup light cream
½ cup chicken broth (or ½ cup water, 1 bouillon)
¾ cup shredded sharp cheese
1 can sliced mushrooms, drained
4 Tablespoons grated Vidalia onion
   Salt
¼ teaspoon paprika
2 Tablespoons white wine, optional
¼ cup bread crumbs

Defrost and drain crab. Melt margarine and stir in flour until smooth. Gradually stir in milk, cream and broth. Cook, stirring constantly, over low heat until sauce is smooth and thick. Add cheese, mushrooms, onion, salt, paprika and wine. Stir until cheese is melted. Stir in chunks of crab. Pour mixture into well-greased casserole. Sprinkle bread crumbs over top. Bake at 350 degrees F. for 20 minutes or until top is golden brown. Serve over hot cooked rice.

 Waste not an onion! Before your Vidalia onions spoil, peel, wash and bake them in a cup of water in baking dish for 30 minutes. Cool, put in freezer bags and freeze.

Grandfather's Farm

I knew every inch of that farm.
I knew where the violets grew.
I knew when the birds passed overhead
And upon which path they flew.

I knew each trail cut through the woods
And the meandering of the stream.
I knew exactly what time of year
The grass began to green.

I knew every stretch of land, oh yes,
I knew its rise and fall.
I knew from which hill the cows
   would come
When they heard the cattle call.

I knew the color of the earth
When it was turned in spring.
I knew the thud of horses hooves
And the harness familiar ring.

I knew the height of the walnut tree.
It almost touched the sky.
I knew what time of evening
To listen for the whippoorwill cry.

I knew where to perch and watch
The lightning bugs bright show.
I knew just when the jasmine bloomed.
And where the wild fern would grow.

I knew what spot the tool box took
On the wall of the old truck shed.
I knew the sound of beating rain
On the tin roof overhead.

I knew every thing there was to know
About how that farm lay.
The only thing I didn't know
Was how easily it could slip away.

Carol Plummer

MEATS

SAUSAGE WITH CABBAGE AND VIDALIA ONIONS
"Great dish for little buddies and big fellows"

2 medium onions, sliced
2 Tablespoons vegetable oil
1 pound Polish sausage, sliced
1 medium cabbage, chopped or cut into small wedges

In a large skillet, cook sliced onions in oil for 5 minutes. Use medium heat. Put the onions in a bowl and in the same oil fry the sausage but do not brown them. Put the cabbage in the skillet with sausage and cook about 5 minutes. Cover the skillet and cook for 3 minutes. Stir in the cooked onions and heat through.

PORK IN PEACH BOATS

1 pound bulk sausage meat
2 Tablespoons minced Vidalia onion
2 cups soft bread crumbs
¼ teaspoon seasoning salt
  Dash of pepper
1 egg, beaten
8 fresh peach halves
  Whole cloves (optional)

Combine and mix well the first six ingredients. Form into balls about 1½ inches in diameter. Wash, peel, cut in half and pit the peaches. Arrange in a shallow glass baking dish. Stick with whole cloves, if desired. Place a sausage ball in pit cavity of each peach. Place remaining sausage balls in baking dish. Bake in 350 degrees F. oven for 45 minutes. When meat is done gently remove peaches and sausage balls to a hot platter or drain off excess juices and serve in the baking dish. Before serving pour hot*Spiced Peach Syrup over the peaches and sausage.

*Spiced Peach Syrup:
  1 cup sugar
  ¼ cup vinegar
  3 whole cloves
  1 stick cinnamon
  1 peach, chopped

Mix all ingredients and boil for 5 minutes. Strain and pour in syrup pitcher for serving.

TASTY CHICKEN BAKE

8 slices bread
1 cup sour cream
  Salt and pepper to taste
1 cup chopped Vidalia onion
½ cup chopped celery
½ cup chopped green pepper
1 jar diced pimento, drained
3 cups chopped, cooked chicken
2 eggs, beaten
1 cup milk
1 can condensed cream of mushroom soup
½ cup shredded Cheddar cheese

Cube four slices of bread and place in bottom of buttered baking dish. In large bowl, combine sour cream with salt and pepper. Add celery, onion, green pepper, pimento and chicken; mix well. Spoon over bread cubes. Trim crusts from remaining slices of bread; place on top of mixture. Combine eggs with milk; pour over all. Cover and chill at least 1 hour or overnight. When ready to bake, spoon soup evenly over top of casserole. Bake in 325 degree F. oven for 50 minutes. Sprinkle cheese on top and continue for 10 minutes or until set. Serve while hot.

TURKEY BAKE WITH VIDALIA ONIONS
"Tasty way to use left over turkey"

1 cup shredded sharp Cheddar cheese
2 cups crushed potato chips
1 Tablespoon butter
4 Tablespoons grated Vidalia onion
½ cup chopped pecans
3 cups cooked, diced turkey
1 cup chopped celery
½ cup mayonnaise
  Lemon juice
  Salt and pepper to taste

Mix cheese and potato chips. Place half of mixture in bottom of greased baking dish.

Melt butter in skillet and cook onion until tender. Combine onion with remaining ingredients and spoon over potato chip mixture. Sprinkle remaining cheese and chip mixture over turkey and bake at 350 degree F. for 20 minutes.

Store Vidalia onions in the refrigerator to keep them for a long period of time or for several weeks. You may wrap each onion with a paper towel. Check them often.

SWEET AND SOUR PORK CHOPS

2 Tablespoons oil
8 pork chops
Salt and pepper to taste
2 large Vidalia onions, sliced
1 small bell pepper, sliced
1 cup pineapple juice
1 can tomato sauce (8 ounces)
2 Tablespoons lemon juice
¼ cup brown sugar

In heavy skillet, brown pork chops in oil. Season with salt and pepper. Place chops in a single layer in a shallow baking dish. Saute' onions and pepper in skillet. Stir in pineapple juice, tomato sauce, lemon juice and sugar; stir constantly until boiling. Pour sauce over pork chops, cover with foil and bake at 325 degrees F. for 1 hour.

MINTED LOIN OF PORK WITH VIDALIA ONIONS

1 loin of pork, boneless
Marinade:
1 medium Vidalia onion, minced
½ cup minced celery
1 leek, minced
1 Tablespoon fresh thyme, crushed
½ teaspoon rosemary
2 Tablespoons parsley, finely chopped
1 Tablespoon crushed black peppercorns
½ Tablespoon sea salt
1 cup olive oil
1 pineapple, peeled, cored and crushed in blender
¼ cup orange zest, plus pulp of 1 orange, chopped
½ cup fresh mint
⅓ cup tomato puree
1 cup Port wine

Combine the marinade ingredients; pour over the loin and marinade overnight. Grill slowly over charcoal grill for 15 minutes, turning every 5 minutes. Remove from grill and finish roasting in 400 degree F. oven until tender. Remove from oven and allow to cool for about 10 minutes. Slice and garnish with sprigs of mint.

REFRIGERATE THOSE VIDALIA ONIONS!
(Use an open box of soda in the refrigerator to absorb the odor.)

STIR-FRY HAM WITH PEACHES AND VIDALIAS

1 can sliced cling peaches, (1 pound, 13 ounces)
¾ cup water
3 Tablespoons dry sherry
3 Tablespoons soy sauce
2 Tablespoons honey
2 Tablespoons cornstarch
¼ teaspoon ginger
2 Tablespoons cooking oil (use peanut oil in a wok)
1 clove garlic, sliced
1 pound fully-cooked ham, thinly sliced
1 cup fresh or frozen peas, thawed
½ cup Vidalia onion, minced
1 can water chestnuts, drained and sliced
3 cups cooked rice

Drain sliced peaches, save ½ cup of syrup. Combine reserved syrup, water, sherry, soy sauce, honey, cornstarch and ginger, mix well. Heat oil and garlic in skillet, saute' garlic; remove oil. Add ham in hot skillet, a few pieces at a time. Cook and stir one minute.

Stir cornstarch mixture and add ham, peas, and onion. Cook, stirring until thickened. Add sliced peaches and water chestnuts; stir slowly to coat with sauce. Heat thoroughly. Serve over cooked rice.

CREAMED TACOS AND SWEET VIDALIAS

1 can cream of mushroom soup
1 can taco sauce (7½ ounces)
1 pound Velveeta cheese, diced
½ can water
2 pounds ground beef
1 large Vidalia onion, chopped
2 teaspoons cumin powder
2 teaspoons salt
Dash of garlic powder
½ teaspoon cayenne pepper
2 Tablespoons flour
1 cup hot water
20-24 tortillas
Vegetable oil

Mix first 3 ingredients and ½ cup soup can of water; cook over low heat until cheese is melted. Cook beef and onion together until lightly browned; add cumin, salt, garlic powder and pepper. Drain off excess fat; stir in flour. Add 1 cup hot water; simmer for 15 minutes. Fry tortillas in hot oil. Place 2 to 3 tablespoons beef mixture on each tortilla; roll. Place in baking dish; pour cheese sauce over tortillas. Bake in 300 degrees F. oven for 20 to 30 minutes.

QUAIL-VIDALIA ONION-PEANUT DRESSING
"Fit for King and Queen"

1 medium Vidalia onion, diced
¾ cup celery, diced
3 Tablespoons peanut oil
2 quarts baked cornbread, crumbled (8 cups)
5 toasted bread slices, crumbled
1 teaspoon salt
1 teaspoon pepper
1 teaspoon poultry seasoning
1 cup roasted peanuts, chopped
2 eggs, slightly beaten
6 Tablespoons butter
8 dressed quail, fresh or frozen
1 quart chicken stock

In heavy skillet saute' onion and celery in peanut oil. Remove from heat and stir in breads, salt, pepper, poultry seasonings, peanuts and eggs. Set aside. Heat 4 Tablespoons of butter in chicken stock until melted. Mix into the bread mixture.

If quail is frozen, thaw. Lightly rub outsides of each bird with 2 tablespoons of butter. Use about 2 cups of dressing to loosely stuff the birds. Place stuffed birds in a 9 x 13 baking pan and cover. Spoon remaining dressing into lightly greased baking dish. Bake dressing and stuffed birds in 350 degree F. oven for 1 hour. Cut dressing into 8 squares. Serve birds on dressing squares.

ROASTED WILD TURKEY

1 turkey, 8 to 10 pounds ready-to-cook
8 cups partially dry bread crumbs
¾ cups finely chopped celery
½ cup chopped walnuts
2 to 3 teaspoons sage
   Salt and pepper to taste
1½ cups Vidalia onion, chopped
¼ cup butter or margarine
2 cups water

Sprinkle turkey inside and out with salt and pepper. Combine bread, celery, walnuts and seasonings. Cook onion in butter or margarine until tender, but not brown; pour over bread mixture. Add the water and toss lightly. Spoon stuffing lightly into body cavity. Put remaining dressing in a greased casserole. Cover and bake in oven with turkey during last 30 minutes of roasting time.

Truss bird. Cover breast with bacon slices and cheesecloth soaked in melted bacon fat. Place turkey, breast up, on rack in roasting pan. Roast at 325 degrees F. 20 to 25 minutes per pound or until tender, basting frequently with bacon fat and drippings in pan. Remove cheesecloth, skewers and string. Serves 8 to 10.

CHICKEN LIVERS WITH VIDALIA ONIONS

1 pound chicken livers, floured
  Salt and pepper to taste
  Vegetable oil
¼ cup butter
1 large Vidalia onion, chopped
½ cup sliced mushrooms
1 Tablespoon sherry

Flour chicken livers. Salt and pepper them. Saute' a few at at time in oil until brown. In another pan, heat butter. Cook chopped onion until clear. Add mushrooms and cook a few minutes. Add the livers and sherry to the pan and simmer about 5 minutes.

BRAISED LIVER AND VIDALIA ONIONS

2 Tablespoons oil
1 pound beef liver, cut into 1-inch pieces
1 small onion, sliced
¼ cup dry sherry
2 Tablespoons chopped parsley (optional)
1 Tablespoon lemon juice
½ teaspoon salt and pepper

Heat oil in skillet over moderate heat. Dredge liver in flour, put in skillet and brown on both sides; add remaining ingredients. Cover and cook about 10 to 12 minutes. Serve with Water Fried Vidalia Onions.

Water Fried Vidalia Onions: Slice 3 large Vidalia onions; place in thick frying pan. Sprinkle with all-purpose seasoning, salt and pepper. Cook over low heat about 2 minutes. When onions begin to carmelize, stir and add ¼ cup water; cover pan and cook until onions are tender.

CHICKEN LIVERS AND MUSHROOMS

1 slice bacon, diced
1 Vidalia onion, diced
1 pound chicken livers
1 pound mushrooms, sliced
2 Tablespoons flour
1 cup chicken broth
½ teaspoon lemon juice
  Salt and pepper to taste

Cook bacon in heavy skillet. Add onion and saute' until tender. Add livers and mushrooms and saute' about 6 minutes or until livers are well browned. Blend flour into drippings. Add remaining ingredients and cook, stirring until thick. Simmer for 3 minutes.

VIDALIA ONION-CHICKEN 'N' BISCUIT POT PIE

2 broiler-fryer chickens (2½ -3 pounds each)
3 cups water
2 teaspoons salt
3 sprigs parsley
3 celery tops with leaves
1 cup celery, sliced
1 carrot, quartered
2 medium onions, chopped (2 cups)
8 peppercorns
2 packages frozen mixed vegetables (10 ounces)
½ cup butter
1 teaspoon thyme leaves
½ cup all-purpose flour
3 cups chicken broth, from simmered chicken
1 cup milk
2 cans refrigerated biscuits (8 ounces)

Rinse chickens in cold water and place in 5-quart kettle with water, salt, parsley, celery tops, carrot, 1 cup onion and peppercorns. Bring to a boil. Reduce heat, cover and simmer about 1 hour, or until tender.

Remove chicken to large platter or pan, cover with foil and place in refrigerator until cool enough to remove meat from skin and bones. Cut into large chunks. Refrigerate.

Strain broth; discard vegetables. Return broth to kettle and boil rapidly, uncovered.

To prepare pot pie: Cook mixed vegetables with ½ cup onions. Drain, set aside.

In skillet melt butter; add 1 cup celery, ½ cup onion and saute' until tender, stirring. Blend flour smoothly. Gradually stir in chicken broth and milk. Cook sauce constantly until mixture comes to a boil. Add chicken, vegetables to sauce; mix well. Butter a 4-quart casserole or large roasting pan. Pour in mixture.

On a floured pastry cloth, roll out biscuits, place on top of mixture. Bake in 400 degree F. oven until biscuits are brown. If you have more biscuits, push the browned biscuits into mixture. Roll out more biscuits, place on top, dot with butter and bake to a golden brown.

LIVER BALLS WITH VIDALIA ONIONS

½ pound liver
1 cup dried bread crumbs
1 Tablespoon flour
2 Tablespoons Vidalia onions, minced
2 eggs, well beaten
Salt and pepper to taste

Parboil liver in boiling water; reserve stock. Put liver through food chopper. Add bread crumbs, flour, onion and seasonings. Mix well and add eggs. If not moist enough to hold together, add a little milk. Drop from tip of spoon into boiling liver stock. Cover and simmer 20 minutes. (Vigorous boiling when balls are first put in might break them.) Serve in plates with soup.

 Check those bags of Vidalia onions. Refrigerate them as soon as possible.

STIR-FRY BEEF-BROCCOLI AND VIDALIA ONIONS

Marinade:
> ¼ cup soy sauce
> 1½ teaspoons sugar
> 2 Tablespoons cornstarch
> ½ teaspoon salt
> 2 Tablespoons cooking sherry

> 1 pound beef top round steak, thinly diagonally sliced
> 2 Tablespoons peanut oil
> 1 clove garlic, crushed
> 1 bunch fresh broccoli
> 1 Vidalia onion, thinly sliced
> Cooked rice

Prepare marinade of soy sauce, sugar, cornstarch, salt and sherry. Add meat; refrigerate for one hour or overnight. Heat wok and add oil and garlic. Cut broccoli into bite-size pieces. Add broccoli and heat until crisp, stirring frequently. Add onion and meat. Heat, stirring until meat begins to change color and onion is crisp. Do not overcook. Simmer for a few seconds and serve over hot rice.

VIDALIA ONIONS APPLES AND CHICKEN LIVERS

> 12 chicken livers (¾ pound)
> 2 Tablespoons flour
> ½ teaspoon salt
> ¼ teaspoon paprika
> 6 Tablespoons butter
> 2 Vidalia onions, cut in thin strips
> 3 cooking apples, cored but unpeeled, sliced
> Parsley for garnish

Cut livers in half, discarding center membranes; dry with paper towel. Dust with a mixture of flour, salt and paprika.

In a large skillet heat 2 tablespoons of the butter; add the onion and cover; cook until soft. Stir them occasionally. Remove them and keep in a warm oven.

Add 2 tablespoons more butter to the skillet, and brown the livers; cook over moderate heat about 10minutes. Remove them to a hot serving platter and keep hot in the oven.

Add the remaining 2 tablespoons of butter to the skillet and fry the apple rings until golden brown but still hold their shape. Spoon the onions over the livers; top with apple rings; and garnish.

 Store your Vidalia onions in the refrigerator. BE SURE TO CHECK THEM OFTEN.

SPINACH BURGERS AND VIDALIA ONIONS

1 package frozen chopped spinach, thawed and drained (10 ounces)
1 pound ground beef
2 eggs, beaten
½ cup Vidalia onion, chopped
½ cup fine dry bread crumbs
1 Tablespoon Worcestershire sauce
1 Tablespoon vegetable oil
½ teaspoon pepper and salt
7 slices Mozzarella cheese
7 hamburger buns, split and toasted

Combine spinach, ground beef, eggs, onion, bread crumbs, sauce, oil, salt and pepper. Shape into patties. Line baking pan with foil. Place patties in pan and broil in oven for 10 to 15 minutes or desired doneness. Top with cheese slices. Serve on toasted buns.

COUNTRY RIBS

5 pounds spare ribs
1 medium Vidalia onion, finely chopped
4 Tablespoons bacon grease or
3 slices finely chopped bacon
1 pint spicy catsup
Juice of 1 lemon
⅓ cup brown sugar
1 teaspoon salt
½ teaspoon chili powder

Lightly brown onion in bacon grease or cook with chopped bacon. Remove from heat. Add catsup, stir. Add remaining ingredients and simmer slowly about 10 minutes. Cook ribs on grill following manufacturer's instructions. When ribs are tender, remove from grill. Brush ribs with cooked sauce.

CHEESE TURKEY LOAF

½ cup sweet Vidalia onion
¼ cup green pepper, chopped
1 can tomato sauce (8 ounces)
2 eggs, beaten
4 ounces process American cheese, diced
1 cup soft bread crumbs
Salt and pepper to taste
¼ teaspoon dried thyme, crushed
2 pounds of ground turkey

Cook onion and green pepper in boiling water until tender; drain. Stir in tomato sauce, eggs, cheese, bread crumbs, salt, pepper and thyme. Add ground turkey mixing well. Shape into loaf in baking dish. Bake in 350 degree F. for 1 hour.

DISHPAN CHICKEN PIE

1 large hen (4 to 6 pounds)
1 fryer chicken, (3 to 4 pounds)
1 cup chopped Vidalia onion
2 teaspoons seasoned salt
1 teaspoon celery seed
2 bay leaves
Pepper to taste
Water

Place hen and fryer in large pot, cover with water. Add onion and seasonings. Cover and cook until chickens are tender. You will have to turn the chickens to keep them from sticking to bottom of pot. Cool. Remove bones and bay leaves. Save the chicken broth for the dishpan recipe-
Pastry:
3 cups self-rising flour
3 cups all-purpose flour
1½ cups shortening
Water to make pastry

Combine flours by sifting together in large mixing bowl. Cut in the shortening with pastry blender. Add enough water to make thick pastry; divide into 3 equal parts and roll on a floured pastry cloth. Roll the pastry to the size of the dishpan but be sure it is about ¼ -inch thick. Pinch off some of the dough if it is too large.

An enamel roaster-pan (8 to 10 inches deep) may be used if an enamel dishpan is not available. In pan alternate chicken and broth with layers of pastry; starting with chicken and broth as first layer. Pastry should just cover the chicken layer. Bake each layer until brown before adding the next layer. (You may brush each layer with melted butter, if desired.) Bake in 425 degree F. oven until the top crust is golden brown.

SMOTHERED CHICKEN WITH VIDALIA ONIONS

⅓ cup flour
½ teaspoon salt
Dash of pepper
1 chicken, cut up (3 pounds)
¼ cup shortening
1 package dried chicken noodle soup mix
1 cup water
1 cup evaporated milk
1 medium Vidalia onion, sliced

Combine flour, salt and pepper in a paper bag. Shake chicken in mixture to coat. In a 10-inch skillet melt shortening and brown chicken slowly. Drain off all drippings and sprinkle soup mix over chicken in skillet. Add water, milk and sliced onion; cover and cook over low heat for 30 minutes, or until chicken is done. Place chicken in serving dish and keep warm. Add flour and milk to liquid in skillet; cook and stir until thickened. Pour gravy over chicken or bed of rice.

CHICKEN AND DUMPLINGS

1 3 pound chicken, cut in pieces
½ cup Vidalia onions, chopped
¼ teaspoon pepper
1 Tablespoon seasoned salt
Dumplings:
2 cups flour
3 teaspoons baking powder
1 teaspoon salt
⅓ cup shortening
½ cup milk

In Dutch oven place chicken and cover with water; add onion and seasonings. Simmer over medium heat for 30 to 40 minutes. Remove chicken and cool. Remove bones and skin. Cut chicken into small pieces and return to broth.

Dumplings: Sift together flour, baking powder, and 1 teaspoon salt; cut in shortening with pastry blender. Add milk and mix to a soft ball. Using a pastry cloth, sprinkle flour lightly on cloth. Place dough on cloth and knead lightly or until smooth. Roll dough to 1/8 inch thick; cut 1 inch by 5 inch strips, (or desired length). Add dough strips to gently boiling broth. Cook uncovered about 15 minutes.

VIDALIA ONION SAGE DUMPLINGS

1¼ cups unbleached white flour
¾ teaspoon salt
½ teaspoon sage, crumbled
1½ teaspoons baking powder
2 Tablespoons shortening
1 egg, beaten
¼ cup finely chopped green onion (see page 78)
½ cup milk
1 cup chopped Vidalia onion
4 cups chicken stock, canned or homemade

In a mixing bowl, combine flour, salt, sage and baking powder. Add the shortening and cut it in until the mixture resembles meal. Stir in the egg, green onion and milk, combine thoroughly.

In a pot large enough to hold the dumplings, allowing for some expansion, cook the cup of onion in the chicken stock. Drop the dumpling dough by ½ teaspoon into slow boiling stock. Cook the dumplings, uncovered for 10 minutes. Cover and cook 15 to 20 more minutes at a simmer, or until done (dumplings will be firm.) Remove from the stock with a slotted spoon and place next to the chicken or turkey on a large, heated serving platter.

DEER ROAST WITH VIDALIA ONIONS

1 deer roast (rump, round, or chuck)
  Salt and pepper to taste
1 can tomatoes
1 medium Vidalia onion, sliced

Salt and pepper roast, flour and brown in pan on top of stove. Brown on all sides. Remove and put in Dutch oven or large casserole dish. Add mashed tomatoes and sliced onion. If needed add water to keep meat from sticking. Cook at 350 degrees F. for 2 to 3 hours.

OVEN-BARBEQUED POT ROAST

1 beef chuck pot roast, cut 2 inches thick (3 pounds)
1 medium sweet Vidalia onion, sliced
⅓ cup vinegar
¼ cup catsup
2 Tablespoons cooking oil
2 Tablespoons soy sauce
1 Tablespoon Worcestershire sauce
1 Tablespoon prepared mustard
1 bay leaf
2 teaspoons whole black peppercorns
1 teaspoon salt
¼ teaspoon garlic powder
1 cup water
4 teaspoons cornstarch

Place meat and onion in dish to marinate. For marinade, mix vinegar, catsup, oil, and seasonings. Pour marinade over meat and refrigerate 3 to 24 hours.

To roast, transfer meat, onion and marinade to shallow baking dish. Cover; roast in moderate oven for 1½ to 2 hours, basting occasionally with marinade. Place meat and onion on serving platter and keep warm.

For gravy, measure pan juices, adding water if necessary to make 1 cup. In small saucepan combine the 1 cup water and cornstarch; stir in the pan juices. Cook and stir 2 minutes more. Slice meat diagonally across grain.

ENCHILADA PIE WITH VIDALIAS

1 medium sweet Vidalia onion, chopped
1 medium green pepper, chopped
3 Tablespoons shortening
1 pound ground beef
  Salt and pepper to taste
1 can cream of mushroom soup
1 package tortillas
2 cups grated cheese

Melt shortening in heavy skillet, saute' onion and green pepper until soft; add beef and seasonings. Brown beef. Remove from heat; stir in soup. Soften tortillas in hot shortening; arrange around sides and on bottom of 9 x 13 inch pan. Layer remaining tortillas, beef mixture and cheese in pan. Bake in 350 degrees F. oven for 25 minutes or until cheese browns.

TURKEY IN WINE WITH VIDALIA ONIONS

2 to 3 pounds turkey wings
2 cups water
1 cup dry white wine
6 whole allspice
1 bay leaf
1 root end of celery stalk, trimmed
1 large Vidalia onion, chopped
1 pound frozen whole small carrots
    Salt and pepper to taste

Separate turkey wings at joints. In slow cooker combine turkey with all remaining ingredients except salt and pepper. Cover. Cook at medium heat for 40 minutes until turkey and vegetables are tender.

Remove meat and vegetables. Mix 2 tablespoons of corn starch to 1 teaspoon of sugar and 2 tablespoons of water, stir into the liquid, add salt and pepper and cook about 10 minutes. Pour sauce over turkey and vegetables.

WONDERFUL ONE-DISH MEAL WITH CABBAGE

6 cups beef broth
2½ pounds boneless beef round or first cut brisket
1 cup chopped Vidalia onion
2 bay leaves
8 medium new potatoes
8 carrots, cut in 4-inch lengths
8 cabbage wedges cut 1-inch thick

In large saucepot bring beef broth to a boil. Add beef, onion and bay leaves. Simmer, covered until meat is tender, about 1½ hours for round and 3 hours for brisket. Remove meat to a serving platter; cover to keep warm. Add potatoes to saucepot; simmer covered until partially cooked, about 5 minutes. Add carrots and cabbage; simmer covered until vegetables are tender, about 10 minutes. Remove with slotted spoon to serving platter.

CHINESE BEEF WITH SWEET VIDALIA ONION

2 medium Vidalia onions, chopped
1 cup chopped celery
2 Tablespoons vegetable oil
2 pounds ground chuck beef
½ cup uncooked rice
1 can cream of mushroom soup
1 can water
3 Tablespoons soy sauce
1 medium can mushrooms, chopped
1 can bean sprouts, drained

In a skillet brown onions and celery in oil. Set aside. Cook chuck and rice until meat is done but not brown. Add onions and celery. Mix mushroom soup and water; add soy sauce and mushrooms. Mix well. Toss in bean sprouts. Pour in casserole and cook at 350 degrees F. for 30 minutes covered. Uncover and cook about 20 minutes longer.

SALADS

COLORFUL VIDALIA ONIONS IN SALADS

Red, green, blue and yellow food color.
Vidalia onions, any size, sliced, chopped or quartered
2 cups hot water

Heat water for 2 minutes in the microwave oven. To color the onions use one-half ounce for light colored onions and one ounce for darker colors to two cups of hot water. Put the cut onion into the colored water for 30 minutes. Remove with a slotted spoon and drain. (The hot water will not change the texture.) Keep onions in the refrigerator until needed for salad.

MARINATED POTATO SALAD

¼ cup corn oil
¼ cup green spring Vidalia onion, chopped
2 Tablespoons white wine vinegar
2 Tablespoons dry white wine
1 Tablespoon chopped parsley
½ teaspoon dried dill weed
¼ teaspoon salt and pepper
2 pounds small red potatoes, cooked and sliced

In large bowl stir together first 7 ingredients. Add potatoes. Gently toss to coat well. Cover; chill. Toss before serving.

RICE SALAD WITH SWEET VIDALIAS

3 Tablespoons olive oil
1 Tablespoon wine vinegar
1 large clove garlic, crushed
1 teaspoon salt
½ teaspoon ground pepper
1 teaspoon dried, chopped oregano leaves
2 Tablespoons large capers
½ lemon, cut peel in slivers, use peel only
½ cup chopped celery
½ cup chopped green pepper
1 dozen black olives, sliced
4 medium tomatoes, peeled, coarsely cut
½ cup chopped Vidalia onion
1 cup freshly cooked cold rice

Prepare salad dressing by combining the first 8 ingredients, shake well. Marinate the celery, green peppers, olives, tomatoes and onion in the dressing for 1 hour or more. When ready to serve, remove the garlic and toss with rice.

RED, WHITE AND BLUE CELEBRATION SALAD
WITH VIDALIA ONIONS

Colored Onions:
  2 cups chopped Vidalia onions
  ¼ ounce red food color
  ¼ ounce blue food color
  3 cups hot water

Pour ¼ ounce of red food color in 1 cup hot water in a glass bowl and 1 cup of chopped onions. Put ¼ ounce blue food color in 1 cup hot water with ½ cup of chopped onions. Put ½ cup chopped onions in 1 cup hot water. Soak for 40 minutes. Drain on paper towels and wipe dry.

  3 ounce package berry blue gelatin
  6 ounce package lemon gelatin
  3 ounce package cherry gelatin
  1 15 ounce can blueberries, drained
  ½ cup sour cream
  2 cups milk
  1 small can crushed pineapple, drained
  3 cups boiling water
    Trifle bowl

Bottom layer: Dissolve berry blue gelatin in 1 cup boiling water. Cool in refrigerator. Add ½ cup of white chopped onions. Add drained blueberries. Pour into bottom of clear trifle bowl.

Middle Layer: Dissolve lemon gelatin in 1 cup boiling water. Cool in a separate bowl in refrigerator. Mix sour cream and milk together, pour into lemon gelatin and refrigerate until it thickens. Pour over the bottom layer when it is sticky to touch. Punch down into middle layer red onions on 1 side and blue onions on the other side. Refrigerate.

Top layer: Dissolve cherry gelatin in 1 cup boiling water. Cool in the refrigerator. Add ½ cup red onions and the small can of pineapple. Pour over the middle layer when it is firm but slightly sticky to the touch. Refrigerate until serving time.

SAVE THOSE VIDALIA ONIONS!

Clean and wash onions, chop and spread on a cookie sheet. Put them into the freezer. After they have frozen, put into freezer bags and seal. Stack flat. When needed for a recipe, break off the desired quantity.

GREEN SALAD DRESSING

1 egg, hard-cooked, chopped
1 teaspoon sugar
3 Tablespoons vinegar
1 teaspoon salt
1 clove garlic
1 cup green Vidalia onion tops, chopped coarsely (page 17)
1 cup parsley
¾ cup salad oil
   Dash of Tabasco

Put all ingredients except salad oil into blender and blend a few seconds. Add salad oil and blend until dressing is smooth. Keep refrigerated. Serve on green salads.

CREAMY CABBAGE SLAW

1 medium cabbage
1 medium Vidalia onion
   Salt and pepper to taste
½ cup sugar
1 cup mayonnaise
¼ cup white vinegar
2 teaspoons horseradish

Shred cabbage very fine. Slice onion very fine and separate into rings. Toss these two together. Salt and pepper to taste. Sprinkle sugar over mixture. Combine mayonnaise, vinegar, horseradish. Pour over cabbage and onion. Toss. Chill before using.

GARDEN SALAD

1 envelope lemon gelatin
½ teaspoon salt, optional
1 cup boiling water
1 cup cold water
4 teaspoons vinegar
⅔ cup quartered cucumber slices
½ cup sliced radishes
2 Tablespoons chopped Vidalia onion

Dissolve gelatin and salt in boiling water. Add cold water and vinegar. Chill until thickened. Fold in vegetables. Pour into 3-cup mold or individual molds. Chill until firm. Unmold. Serve on crisp lettuce.

When selecting the best Vidalia onions look for onions that have no blemishes. There should be no sprouts and the skin firm and tight, not excessively dry.

EGG SALAD BLOSSOM CUPS

½ cup chopped Vidalia onion
1 cup mayonnaise
2 Tablespoons lemon juice
½ teaspoon dill weed and salt
1 package frozen, chopped broccoli, thawed and drained
1 package frozen tiny shrimp, thawed and drained
3 hard-cooked eggs, chopped
¼ cup sliced almonds
1 package refrigerated biscuits

Blend together onion, mayonnaise, lemon juice, dill weed and salt. Add broccoli, shrimp, eggs and almonds. Toss, cover and refrigerate to blend flavors.
Separate biscuit dough rounds. Turn the muffin tin pan over and grease the bottom cups. Place 1 round on each of the cups. Pat dough evenly on tops and down sides. Bake in preheated 450 degree F. oven until brown, about 5 minutes. Remove biscuit cups and allow to cool on wire rack. Fill each cup with shrimp and onion mixture.

SEAFOOD SALAD

1½ cups macaroni
½ teaspoon dry mustard
3 hard-cooked eggs
1 can tuna (6½ ounces)
1 can crabmeat (6½ ounces)
2 dill pickles, chopped
¾ cup chopped celery
2 carrots, grated
¼ green pepper, chopped
1 Tablespoon fresh lemon juice
1 cup mayonnaise

Cook macaroni using directions on package. Drain and rinse in cold water. Add remaining ingredients, tossing to mix well. Chill 2 hours or longer.

SHRIMP SALAD

¼ cup tarragon vinegar
1 Tablespoon mustard
1 Tablespoon catsup
½ cup mayonnaise
1 teaspoon paprika
¼ teaspoon salt
¼ cup chopped celery
¼ cup chopped Vidalia onion
2 pounds shrimp, cleaned and cooked

Combine vinegar, mustard, catsup, mayonnaise and spices. Mix thoroughly, then add celery and onion. Pour over shrimp and toss. Refrigerate several hours before serving.

Garnish with colorful yellow and pink onion rings, page 65.

PHEASANT SALAD
"Fit for a King"

1½ cups cold cooked pheasant or chicken cut in small cubes
4 seedless oranges, peeled and sectioned
1 sweet Vidalia onion, thinly sliced
4 Tablespoons chopped fresh mint
¼ cup olive oil
1 Tablespoon orange juice
1 clove garlic, crushed
¼ teaspoon salt
¼ teaspoon pepper
  Salad greens

Mix the pheasant, oranges, onions and mint in a bowl. Blend the oil, orange juice and seasoning together and shake well in a bottle. Pour over the pheasant mixture enough dressing to coat it well and toss lightly. Chill and let mixture marinate in the dressing for an hour or so before serving in a bowl lined with salad greens or lettuce.

SOUR CREAM POTATO SALAD

1½ cups mayonnaise
1 carton sour cream (8 ounces)
1½ teaspoons prepared horseradish
1 teaspoon celery seed
8 medium potatoes, cooked, peeled and sliced
1 cup fresh minced parsley, divided
¾ cup Vidalia onion, chopped and divided

Combine mayonnaise, sour cream, horseradish and celery seed. Set aside. Place half of sliced potatoes in a mixing bowl; sprinkle with ⅓ cup parsley and ¼ cup onion. Top with half of mayonnaise mixture. Repeat layers. Use remaining parsley and onion to garnish top. Cover and chill before serving.

HOMINY SALAD WITH VIDALIA ONIONS

4 slices bacon
½ large onion, thinly sliced
1 can gold hominy (1 pound)
1 cup thinly sliced celery
1 cup chopped green pepper
½ cup chopped red bell pepper
  Salt and pepper to taste

In a skillet, fry bacon crisp, drain on paper towel; crumble. In bacon drippings saute' onions until soft. In large salad bowl mix all ingredients together with seasonings. Use favorite dressing.

If you have a portion of a Vidalia onion left over from a recipe, put it in a freezer bag and freeze for stews and soups.

VIDALIA ONION SUMMER SALAD

1 cup melon balls (or mixed Fruit balls)
1 tomato, peeled and cut into wedges
1½ quarts torn salad greens
¼ cup salad oil
1½ Tablespoons fresh lemon juice
1 Tablespoon minced onion
½ teaspoon Worcestershire sauce
¾ teaspoon salt
½ teaspoon sugar

Combine melon, tomato, greens in salad bowl. Put remaining ingredients into small bowl and stir well. Add to salad and toss.

HOT SALAD WITH VIDALIAS

5 slices bacon, fried and chipped
¼ cup white vinegar
2 Tablespoons water
½ teaspoon sugar
   Pepper and salt to taste OR
   No salt all-purpose seasonings
2½ quarts torn romaine lettuce, curly mustard or
   your favorite salad greens
1 large Vidalia onion sliced
½ cup roasted peanuts

Fry bacon, drain, chip and set aside. In same skillet heat together vinegar, water, sugar and seasoning. Boil about 2 minutes. Pour hot mixture over salad greens, nuts and bacon.

APPLE TUNA SALAD

1 package of lemon gelatin (3 ounces)
1 cup boiling water
1 cup cold water
2 Tablespoons lemon juice
   Dash of pepper
1 can tuna, drained and flaked (7 ounces)
½ cup chopped, unpeeled red apple
¼ cup minced Vidalia onion
1 Tablespoon chopped parsley

Dissolve gelatin in boiling water. Add cold water, lemon juice, and pepper. Chill unil thickened. Fold in tuna, apple. onion, and parsley. Pour into a 4-cup mold. Chill until firm - about 3 hours. Unmold, Serve with salad greens.

Use red and green Vidalia onion rings, recipe *Colorful Vidalia Onions, page 65 in Holiday Pasta recipes.

BAKED CHICKEN SALAD AND VIDALIAS

4 cups crushed potato chips
2 cups cooked and diced chicken
1½ cups sliced celery
½ cup mayonnaise
1 cup cubed Cheddar cheese
1 slice of lemon
½ small onion
¼ cup almonds

Grease a 2-quart casserole dish with margarine. Crush potato chips. Place chicken and celery into casserole. Put mayonnaise, cheese, lemon and onion into blender, cover and process until smooth. Add almonds, process until chopped. Pour over chicken and celery mix. Sprinkle potato chip crumbs over top and bake in 350 degree F. oven for 30 minutes.

BEAN SPROUT ALMOND SALAD

2 cups fresh or canned bean sprouts, rinsed and drained
½ cup sliced celery
½ cup sliced almonds, toasted
2 Tablespoons chopped green pepper
2 Tablespoons chopped sweet Vidalia onion
¼ cup mayonnaise
1 Tablespoon lime or lemon juice
1 teaspoon sugar
½ teaspoon paprika
   Dash of ginger
   Lettuce

In a large bowl combine all ingredients except lettuce. Toss to mix thoroughly. Chill. Line serving platter with lettuce leaves; top with bean sprout mixture.

VIDALIA ONION SPINACH SALAD

1 package frozen chopped spinach
1 sweet onion, chopped
4 Tablespoons butter
   Salt to taste
½ cup sour cream
1 teaspoon vinegar

Cook spinach with onion; drain. Melt butter; add drained spinach and mix well. Stir in remaining ingredients. DELICIOUS!

ROCK SHRIMP SALAD

1½ pounds rock shrimp, headed, peeled, deveined
    boiled and chopped
2 hard-cooked eggs, chopped
¼ cup chopped celery
2 Tablespoons sweet pickle relish
¼ cup chopped sweet Vidalia onion
3 Tablespoons mayonnaise
1 teaspoon lemon juice
    Salt and pepper to taste

Mix all ingredients. Garnish with lemon wedges. Serve on lettuce with crackers. May be prepared ahead of time. Keep refrigerated.

Boiled Rock Shrimp:
    1 quart water
    3 bay leaves
    1 Tablespoon salt and pepper mixed
        Juice of 1 lemon
    1 pound rock shrimp, headed, peeled and deveined

Bring water, bay leaves, salt and pepper to boil. Add lemon juice and shrimp. Cook only 40 seconds. Remove immediately. Drain and rinse with cold water.

LAYERED SALAD WITH SWEET VIDALIA ONIONS

1 head lettuce, well drained
1 green pepper, sliced into rings
1 large sweet onion, sliced
1 can sweet peas. drained
1 cup diced celey
1 pound crisp, fried bacon, crumbled
½ pint mayonnaise
1 cup sour cream
2 Tablespoons sugar
    Salt and pepper to taste
½ pound Cheddar cheese, grated
½ cup chopped roasted peanuts

Break lettuce in small pieces, place in bottom of large salad bowl. Cover with layer of green pepper, onion rings, peas, celery and bacon. Mix mayonnaise, sour cream, sugar and spices together. Smooth mixture over top of layered vegetables. Sprinkle cheese over mixture. Refrigerate for several hours. Sprinkle chopped peanuts on top before serving.

VIDALIA ONION VINEGAR

1 quart chopped Vidalia onions
1 Tablespoon salt
1 pint white vinegar
½ cup sugar

Chop onions very fine and sprinkle with salt. Allow onions to stand 6 hours. Cook sugar in vinegar over medium heat until sugar is dissolved. Put onions in sterilized canning jar; pour vinegar mixture over onions, tighten sterilized lid. Keep in cool place for 16 days. Strain and pour into sterilized bottles. Keep refrigerated.

CABBAGE AND CARROT SLAW

2 cups cabbage, finely shredded
1 cup carrots, shredded
¼ cup green onions, thinly sliced
⅓ cup vinegar
3 Tablespoons sugar
¼ teaspoon garlic powder
¼ teaspoon oregano
¼ teaspoon dry mustard

Combine cabbage, carrots and onions in a 2-quart non-metalic container with a cover. To make dressing, mix remaining ingredients together until sugar is dissolved. Pour dressing over vegetables and mix well. Cover and refrigerate for 4 hours or overnight.

SPINACH-VIDALIA ONION SALAD MOLD

1 box lemon jello (3 ounces)
1 cup boiling water
½ cup cold water
½ cup mayonnaise
1½ Tablespoons vinegar
1 Tablespoon sour cream
¼ teaspoon salt
  Dash of pepper
1 cup raw chopped spinach
¾ cup cottage cheese
⅓ cup diced celery
1 Tablespoon chopped sweet Vidalia onion

Dissolve jello in boiling water. Add cold water, mayonnaise, vinegar, sour cream, salt and pepper. Chill until firm. Beat until fluffy and fold in rest of ingredients. Pour into a four-cup mold; chill until firm. Unmold, and garnish with tomatoes.

EASY CHICKEN SALAD

2 cups cooked chicken or turkey
1 cup finely diced celery
2 Tablespoons diced Vidalia onion
2 Tablespoons chopped pimento
2 Tablespoons fresh lemon juice
½ cup chopped roasted peanuts
¼ teaspoon black pepper
¼ cup mayonnaise

Toss all ingredients together to mix well. Serve as sandwich, stuffed in tomato half or heat ingredients to boiling, serve on *Toast Points or over noodles.

Toast Points:
  Use thin wheat bread. Trim the edges of the bread with a knife and cut into triangles. Bake at 300 degrees F. until slightly brown or dry.

Enjoy red and blue Vidalia onions, recipe *Colorful Vidalia Onions, page 65, in patriotic pasta recipes.

SEAFOOD

PESCADO EN SALSA VERDE
"Fish and green sauce"

1-2 pounds fish (in slices or fillets)
½ cup cooking oil
1 Vidalia onion, chopped
½ cup parsley
  Salt
1 Tablespoon vinegar
½ cup dry wine

Put all ingredients into blender , except fish, and blend. Put fish in frying pan and cover with green sauce. Let it boil two minutes and then cover the pan. Cook over low heat for 15 minutes.

SWEET ONION STUFFED FISH

1 cup finely chopped Vidalia onion
½ cup finely chopped celery
4 Tablespoons butter, melted
  Salt and pepper
2 cups dry bread crumbs
½ teaspoon seasoned salt
2 fish steaks
1 Tablespoon lemon juice

Saute' onion and celery in butter until tender. Add bread crumbs; cook until lightly browned. Add seasonings.

Wipe fish with a damp cloth and sprinkle with salt, pepper and lemon juice. Place half the fish in a buttered baking dish. Spread stuffing over top. Top with remaining fish steak. Brush with melted butter.

Bake in oven for 35 minutes at 350 degrees F. Delicious and so good for your health.

SHRIMP BUTTER

1 pound shrimp, boiled, cleaned and finely chopped
1 8-ounce package cream cheese and 1 stick butter, softened
½ cup minced Vidalia onion and ¼ cup chopped celery
2 Tablespoons mayonnaise and lemon juice
  Salt and pepper to taste (or Creole seasoning)

Blend all ingredients. Chill for 3 hours. Serve on crackers.

BASIC BROILED FISH

2 pounds fat or lean fish fillets or steaks, fresh or frozen
2 Tablespoons melted margarine or cooking oil
2 Tablespoons lemon juice
1 teaspoon salt
½ teaspoon paprika
Dash of pepper

Thaw fish if frozen. Cut fillet into serving size portions. Place fish in a single layer, skin side up, on a well-greased baking pan, 15 x 10 inches. Combine remaining ingredients and mix well. Pour *Spicy Sauce over fish. Broil about 4 inches from heat for 4 to 6 minutes. Turn carefully and baste with sauce. Broil 4 to 6 minutes longer or until fish flakes easily when tested with a fork.

*Spicy Sauce:
⅓ cup steak sauce
¼ cup catsup
¼ cup melted margarine or cooking oil
1 Tablespoon vinegar
1 teaspoon salt
2 Tablespoons grated Vidalia onion (use juice also)

Combine all ingredients and mix well. Makes enough to baste 2 pounds fish fillet.

THE CAPTAIN'S CHOICE

2 pounds fish fillets, fresh or frozen
1 teaspoon salt
¼ teaspoon pepper
½ cup salad dressing or mayonnaise
2 Tablespoons catsup
2 teaspoons prepared mustard

Thaw fish if frozen. Cut filllets into serving size portions. Sprinkle fillets with salt and pepper. Place fish, skin side down, on a well-greased bake and serve platter. Broil fillets about 4 inches from heat for 10 minutes. combine salad dressing, catsup and mustard. Spread mixture evenly over fillets. Broil 4 to 5 minutes longer or until sauce bubbles and is lightly browned. Serve with Vidalia Onion Rings, page 25.

BAKED TROUT

1 trout (2 pounds)
Juice of ½ lemon
Seasoning salt
Lemon slices
Sweet Vidalia onion slices
Butter
Dry parsley

Clean fish, leaving on head and tail if desired. Squeeze lemon juice over fish. Place salt, lemon slice, onion slices and pats of butter on fish. Sprinkle with parsley flakes. Bake in a 325 degree F. oven for 1 hour or until fish is firm.

GRILLED WHOLE SALMON

1 whole salmon or other roundfish (approximately 4-6 pounds)
   Salt and pepper to taste
   Equal amounts of dried marjoram, savory and thyme
   Lemon slices
   Medium Vidalia onion, cut into wedges, then split lengthwise
3-5 sprigs of parsley
   Vegetable oil

Scale and eviscerate salmon; remove gills. Cut off pectoral and pelvic fins and trim tail. Rinse salmon with cold water; pat dry with paper towels. Make three shallow diagonal slashes into each side of salmon. Combine salt, pepper, marjoram, savory and thyme, crushing herbs slightly. Rub mixture into belly cavity and on skin, taking care to rub into slashes. Fill belly cavity with lemon, Vidalia onion and parsley; skewer closed. Baste salmon with vegetable oil. Place in well-greased hinged wire basket and cook 4-5 inches from hot coals. Allow 10 minutes per inch of salmon measured at its thickest point. Baste and turn midway through cooking time. When salmon is browned, test for doneness. Ease onto serving platter. Serve plain or with *Sour Cream Cucumber Sauce. Allow ¾ - 1 pound of whole fish per serving.

*Sour Cream Cucumber Sauce:

1 cucumber, peeled, seeded and chopped
   (approximately 1 cup)
¾ cup sour cream
   Salt and pepper to taste
3 Tablespoons chopped Vidalia onion
1 teaspoon minced parsley
1 teaspoon lemon juice
   Pinch of dill weed

Combine all ingredients and process in blender. Chill for 30 minutes to blend flavors.

CREAM CHEESE STUFFED SALMON STEAKS

6 salmon steaks, one inch thick
4 ounces low-fat cream cheese
2 Tablespoons grated Parmesan cheese
1 Tablespoon chopped parsley
1 Tablespoon chopped fresh basil OR
1 teaspoon dried basil
2 Tablespoons chopped sweet Vidalia onion
3 Tablespoons butter, melted
2 Tablespoons lemon juice
   Salt and pepper to taste
   Toothpicks

Rinse salmon with cold water; pat dry with paper towels. Through the round part of each salmon steak, make a cut to the center bone, creating a pocket for stuffing. Set aside. Combine cheese, parsley, basil and sweet onion; blend well. Divide into six equal portions. Form each portion into a flat oval. Place one oval into pocket in each steak. Fasten openings closed with toothpicks. Place salmon on well-greased broiler pan. Combine butter, lemon juice, salt and pepper. Baste salmon with butter mixture. Broil 4-5 inches from source of heat or 4-5 minutes; turn. Baste and cook an additional 4-5 minutes, or until salmon flakes easily when tested with a fork. Makes 6 servings.

SMOKED BROILED MULLET

2 pounds mullet fillets or other fish
⅓ cup soy sauce
3 Tablespoons cooking oil
1 Tablespoon hickory smoke salt
1 medium Vidalia onion, finely chopped
½ teaspoon paprika
½ teaspoon salt
    Lemon wedges for garnish

Thaw fish if frozen. Skin fillets. Cut fillets into serving-size portions. Combine remaining ingredients except lemon wedges and mix thoroughly. Place fish on a well-greased broiler pan; brush with sauce. Broil about 3 inches from source of heat for 4 to 5 minutes. Turn carefully and brush other side with sauce. Broil 5 minutes longer, basting occasionally. serve with lemon wedges.

STEAMED SHAD WITH MELTED BONES

1 whole shad, cleaned (3 pounds)
2 small bay leaves, crumbled
2 cloves minced garlic
1½ cups white wine
    Salt and pepper to taste
1 Tablespoon cornstarch
1 cup each chopped celery, carrot and onion

Rinse and dry the fish, rub inside and out with salt and pepper and arrange on a rack in a pan with a tight-fitting lid. With the wine add enough water so that it does not touch the fish on the rack. Spread the vegetables over fish, cover the pan with aluminum foil and fit on the lid. Steam over low heat for 5 hours, basting frequently. Put fish in serving dish that can be kept warm. Strain pan liquid, stir in cornstarch mixed with small amount of water until lump-free. Put it in liquid, stirring over medium heat until sauce is smooth. Serve sauce over fish.

GEORGIA CRAB QUICHE

1 cup fresh, cooked crabmeat, flaked
1 cup shredded Swiss cheese
1 deep dish 9-inch pastry shell, unbaked
2 medium Vidalia onions, sliced
3 eggs, beaten
1 cup half and half cream
¼ teaspoon salt and pepper
½ teaspoon grated lemon peel
¼ cup chopped pecans

Sprinkle cheese in bottom of pastry shell. Then add crabmeat and onions. Combine remaining ingredients, except pecans and pour over crabmeat. Top with pecans. Bake at 350 degrees F. for 30 minutes or until set. Let stand 5 to 10 minutes before serving.

STORE VIDALIA ONIONS IN REFRIGERATOR! Enjoy those sweet onions for a long time by putting them in the vegetable section in the refrigerator. Check them often.

QUICK BAKED FISH

2 large halibut steaks, ½ inch thick
½ cup milk
1½ cups crushed corn flakes
2 Tablespoons butter, melted
3 teaspoons salt

Dip halilbut steaks in salted milk. Coat with crushed corn flakes. Place on greased baking sheet. Drizzle with butter. Bake in hot oven 10 minutes, until fish flakes when tested with a fork. Serve with *Hot Tartare Sauce

*Tartare Sauce:
    1 Tablespoon melted butter
    1 Tablespoon flour
    ½ cup milk
    ⅓ cup mayonnaise
    1 teaspoon vinegar
    2 Tablespoons chopped olives
    2 Tablespoons chopped dill pickles
    2 Tablespoons minced Vidalia onion

Melt butter, add flour and blend. Gradually add milk and cook until smooth. Add remaining ingredients. Heat thoroughly. Makes ¾ cup.

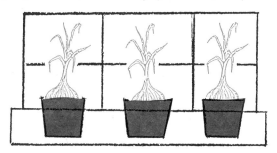

SAVE THOSE VIDALIA ONIONS. If you have onions to sprout, place them in a pot of soil with half of the onions uncovered; water them and put the pots in sunlight. They will grow green sprouts and you will have green onions for several weeks. Cut off a portion of sprouts you need for a recipe. The remaining sprouts will continue to grow. Use some of the sprouts in -
*Green Onion Butter:
    ½ cup butter, softened
    ½ cup Vidalia green onion sprouts, minced
    1 clove garlic, minced
      Pepper to taste
      Dash of hot sauce

Cream butter; add remaining ingredients, beating well. Cover and refrigerator over night for flavors to blend. Use on grilled steaks, baked fish or bread.

STUFFED FLOUNDER

1 flounder ready to cook (4 pounds)
¼ cup finely chopped Vidalia onion
¼ package stuffing mix
½ pound crabmeat
1 Tablespoon lemon juice
4 strips bacon

Cut a pocket on each side of backbone. Mix onion, stuffing, crabmeat and lemon juice. Stuff the pockets and place bacon across the stuffed pockets. Bake in greased baking dish 40 minutes at 350 degrees F. or according to thickness of the fish.

BROILED FLOUNDER FILLETS

2 pounds fresh or frozen flounder fillets
2 Tablespoons lemon juice
3 Tablespoons mayonnaise
½ cup grated Parmesan cheese
3 Tablespoons chopped Vidalia onion
  Salt and pepper to taste
3 Tablespoons butter

Thaw frozen fish. Place a layer on a greased baking dish. Brush fillets with lemon juice and let stand for 10 minutes. Combine remaining ingredients. Broil fillets 4 inches from source of heat for 6 minutes or until fish flakes easily when tested. Spread cheese mixture over the fillets. Broil until light brown.

FOIL BAKED FISH FILLETS

¼ cup oil or margarine
¼ cup chopped sweet Vidalia onion and green peppers
1 package frozen corn, thawed (10 ounces)
1 teaspoon all-purpose seasoning (no-salt)
4 flounder fillets (1 pound)

In heavy skillet melt margarine, saute' onion and green peppers. Add corn and seasoning. Cook, stirring until heated. Line baking pan with foil; place fish on foil. Divide mixture evenly on fillets. Dot with margarine. Place foil on top and crimp edges tightly. Bake in 350 degrees F. oven for 20 minutes.

VIDALIA ONION MARINDADE

1 medium onion, chopped
2 cups red wine and 2 cups vinegar
2 whole cloves and 1 bay leaf
½ teaspoon garlic, salt and lemon pepper

Mix all ingredients and keep refrigerated until used.

SAVORY BAKED MULLET WITH VIDALIA ONIONS

2 pounds mullet fillets, fresh or frozen
2 teaspoons lemon juice
  Pepper to taste
6 slices bacon
1 thinly sliced Vidalia onion
1½ cups soft bread crumbs
2 Tablespoons chopped parsley

Thaw fish if frozen. Skin fillets. Place them in a greased baking dish, 12 x 8 inches. Sprinkle with fresh lemon juice and pepper. Fry bacon until crisp, remove from fat and crumble. Cook onion in bacon fat until tender. Remove from fat and arrange onion evenly over fillets. Combine bacon, bread crumbs, parsley. Sprinkle mixture over fillets. Bake in moderate oven, 350 degrees F. for 25 minutes or until fish flakes easily when tested with a fork.

SCALLOPED TUNA

1 large can tuna
2 Tablespoons vegetable oil
½ cup chopped Vidalia onion
3 Tablespoons all-purpose flour
½ teaspoon salt
¼ teaspoon pepper
¼ teapoon powered thyme
1½ cups liquid non-fat milk
1 box frozen green beans, cooked
½ cup celery, diced fine

Drain tuna. Coarsely chop tuna. In skillet, heat 2 tablespoons oil, saute' onions and blend in flour and seasonings. Slowly add milk. Cook, stirring until thickened. Add tuna and vegetables and mix well. Turn into 1½ -quart baking dish. Bake in preheated moderate oven 350 degrees F. for 30 minutes.

BAKED COD FISH FILLETS

2 pounds cod fillets (if frozen, thaw)
2 Tablespoons all-purpose flour
1 small sweet Vidalia onion, sliced
1 can tomatoes, (1 pound)
1 pimento, chopped
1 bay leaf
1 teaspoon salt
  Dash of pepper and oregano

Cut fillets into serving pieces and put in shallow 2-quart baking dish. Mix remaining ingredients and pour over fish. Bake in preheated 350 degree F. oven for about 1 hour.

COCONUT FRIED SHRIMP

1 pound raw shrimp, shelled and deveined
¼ cup lemon juice
½ teaspoon salt
¼ teaspoon ginger
3 teaspoons curry powder
1¾ cups flour
2 teaspoons baking powder
2 Tablespoons minced Vidalia onion
1¼ cups skimmed milk
½ cup cream of coconut
3½ ounce can flaked coconut
   Vegetable oil

Marinate shrimp in lemon juice, salt, ginger and curry powder for 2 hours. Drain well. Prepare batter of 1½ cups flour, baking powder, onion, milk and cream of coconut. Coat shrimp with remaining flour; dip in prepared batter and dip lightly into flaked coconut. Fry about 6 shrimp at a time in deep fat for 2 to 3 minutes.

MARINATED SHRIMP AND VIDALIA ONIONS

4 pounds shrimp
2 large sweet Vidalia onions, sliced
1½ cups vinegar
1 Tablespoon whole cloves
1 Tablespoon crushed peppercorns
1 stick cinnamon bark
1½ cups oil
¾ cup fresh lemon juice
1 Tablespoon dill seed
1 teaspoon celery seed
   Pepper sauce to taste

Peel and devein shrimp; steam 8 to 10 minutes. Cut onions in rings, put in cold ice water. Mix all other ingredients in a sauce pan and simmer about 10 minutes. Place shrimp and onion in large salad bowl; pour cooked mixture over them. Let stand in refrigerator for several hours or overnight.

VIDALIA ONIONS IN SHRIMP GRAVY

2 slices bacon
1 large green pepper, diced
1 medium Vidalia onion, chopped
¼ cup milk
2 cans cream of chicken soup
1 Tablespoon Worcestershire sauce
1½ cups diced shrimp
   Salt and pepper to taste

Cook bacon until crisp and drain on paper towels. Add pepper and onion and saute until soft. Add milk and soup. Lower the heat and simmer for 20 minutes; stir often. Add sauce and shrimp and cook unitl shrimp are done. May add salt and pepper to taste. Serve over cooked rice.

CATFISH WITH VIDALIA ONIONS AND SALSA

3 to 5 catfish fillets rolled in cornmeal
1/4 cup peanut oil
1 medium Vidalia onion, chopped
2 garlic cloves, minced
3 fresh jalapeno chilies, seeded and minced
3 ripe tomatoes, peeled, seeded and diced
1/2 cup coarsely chopped roasted peanuts
1 Tablespoon lime juice
1/4 cup chopped cilantro
1/2 teaspoon salt
1/4 teaspoon freshly ground black pepper

In a large fry pan over medium high heat, cook the catfish in the peanut oil for 4 to 6 minutes or until done. Remove and keep warm. Add onion and garlic to the pan and saute' over medium heat until tender; about 10 minutes. Add chilies, tomatoes, and peanuts, cook for 5 minutes. Stir in lime juice, cilantro, salt and pepper. Serve the salsa with the catfish.

CRAB QUICHE

1/2 cup mayonnaise
2 Tablespoons flour
2 eggs, beaten
1/2 cup milk
1 cup crabmeat
1/2 pound Swiss cheese, cubed
1/3 cup chopped Vidalia onion
1 deep-dish pie shell

Bake pie shell until slightly brown. Combine mayonnaise, flour, eggs, milk and mix together. Stir in crabmeat, cheese and onion. Spoon into pie shell and bake at 350 degrees F. 30 to 40 minutes until firm in the center.

CRAB SHELLS STUFFED WITH VIDALIAS

1 stick butter
1 Vidalia onion, chopped
1/2 green pepper, chopped
1/4 cup minced shallots
1/2 cup celery, chopped
1/2 loaf bread, cubed
    Salt, red and black pepper to taste
1/4 cup chopped parsley
1 pound lump crabmeat

Saute' onion, green pepper, shallots and celery in butter until soft and well cooked. Add bread, parsley and seasonings. Saute' well while stirring. Allow stuffing to cool and then add crabmeat. Fill cleaned crab shells and top with buttered crumbs. Bake at 375 degrees F. until brown on top.

**KEEP THOSE VIDALIA ONIONS COOL AND REFRIGERATED.
CHECK THEM OFTEN!**

BAKED SHARK WITH VEGETABLES

1½ pounds shark fillets, fresh or frozen
½ teaspoon salt
¼ teaspoon pepper
1 can mixed vegetables, drained (16 ounces)
   Parsley for garnish
   *Onion Sauce

Thaw fish if frozen. Skin fillet; cut into serving-size pieces. Place fish in a single layer in a well-greased, 1½-quart shallow casserole. Sprinkle with salt and pepper. In a 1-quart bowl, combine vegetables with *Onion Sauce. Spread over fish. Cover and bake at 350 degrees F. 20 to 25 minutes or until fish flakes easily when tested with a fork. Garnish with parsley.

*Onion Sauce:
   2 Tablespoons margarine
   ¼ cup grated Vidalia onion
   2 Tablespoons flour
   1 cup milk
   Salt and pepper to taste

In heavy skillet, melt margarine and saute' onion until tender. Add flour; stir slowly until smooth. Gradually add milk, salt. Cook unitil sauce thickens.

CRAB CAKE TREATS WITH VIDALIAS

3 Tablespoons butter
¾ cup finely chopped Vidalia onion
1 cup soft bread crumbs
1 pound crab meat, flaked, bony tissue removed
3 eggs, beaten
¾ teaspoon salt
1 teaspoon dry mustard
1/8 teaspoon paprika
1 teaspoon Worcestershire sauce
3 Tablespoons chopped parsley
2 Tablespoons cream
½ cup flour
   Vegetable oil or butter

In a heavy skillet melt butter and partially cook onion. Remove from heat and stir in bread crumbs. Combine with the crab meat. Add a mixture of the beaten eggs, salt, mustard, paprika, Worcestershire sauce and parsley; blend well. Add enough cream to hold the crabmeat mixture together. Shape into 12 cakes. Coat cakes with flour. Fry in butter or oil until cakes are golden brown and cooked through; about 3 minutes on each side. Serve with lemon wedges. Delicious!

 To peel a large quantity of onions, cover them with hot water for 3 to 5 minutes. The skins will come off easily.

PICKLES AND SAUCES

ICICLE PICKLES

3 pounds cucumbers (4 inches long)
6 small Vidalia onions, peeled, quartered
6 pieces celery (5 inches long)
1 Tablespoon mustard seed
1 quart white vinegar
2½ cups sugar
¼ cup salt
1 cup water

Wash cucumbers; cut into eighths lengthwise. Soak in ice water 3 hours. Drain; pack in clean pint jars. Add 1 onion, 1 piece celery and ½ teaspoon mustard seed to each jar. Combine vinegar and remaining ingredients; bring to boil. Pour solution over cucumbers, filling jar to ½ - inch from top. Immediately adjust covers as jar maunufacturer directs. Process in *Boiling Water Bath for 10 minutes) see below. Makes 6 pints.

*Boiling Water Bath:

1. In a deep kettle or canner, place filled jars on wire rack and cover. (If no rack is available, folded chicken wire, or wooden clothes pins may be placed in the bottom of canner.)
2. Add enough boiling water to cover tops of jars 1 inch; place over heat.
3. When water comes to a rolling boil again, start counting processing time. Keep water boiling steadily.
4. At end of processing time, remove jars; adjust seal by following instructions which come with jar lids. Place jars upright, well apart on a cake rack or thick folded towel. Keep out of draft.
5. The next day, test seal of jars. If jars are not sealed, refrigerate and serve within several days.

Water bath ca

Rack

PICKLED VIDALIA ONIONS

3 pounds small onions, pickling size (1½ quarts)
½ cup salt
1 cup sugar
1 Tablespoon mustard seed
3 cups white vinegar (use good grade)
3 small red peppers
3 bay leaves

Scald onions 2 minutes in boiling water; submerge in cold water; peel. Sprinkle with salt. Add cold water to cover. Let stand at least 12 hours. Drain; rinse; drain. Combine sugar, mustard seed and vinegar; simmer 5 minutes. Meanwhile, pack onions into hot, sterilized jars. Place 1 red pepper and 1 bay leaf in each jar. Pour boiling liquid over onions to within 1/8 inch from top, making sure onions are covered. Quickly seal each jar. Makes 3 pints. Process in boiling water bath for 10 minutes, page 84.

CUCUMBER ONION MUSTARD PICKLES

6 pounds pickling cucumbers (3 to 4 inches long)
1 pound Vidalia onions, pickling size
⅓ cup each sugar and salt
2 Tablespoons cornstarch
1½ teaspoons powdered alum
1 teaspoon ground ginger
½ teaspoon tumeric
¼ teaspoon pepper
2 Tablespoons prepared mustard
3 cups white vinegar (good grade)
1 cup water

Wash cucumbers, scrub with vegetable brush, clean thoroughly; slice. Combine sugar and next 6 ingredients in deep saucepot. Gradually stir in mustard, the liquids. Cover; bring to a boil. Add vegetables. Cover, heat just to boiling point; then simmer while quickly packing one hot, sterilized jar at a time. Fill to within 1/8 inch from top, making sure vinegar solution covers vegetables. Seal each jar at once. Makes 8 pints. Process in boiling water bath for 10 minutes, page 84.

RUMMAGE PICKLES

3 large Vidalia onions, peeled and chopped
1 small cabbage, core removed and chopped
2 quarts green tomatoes, chopped
1 quart red tomatoes, peeled and chopped
1 large ripe cucumber, diced
3 small bunches celery, sliced
3 red peppers, seeded and chopped
3 green peppers, seeded and chopped
½ cup salt
3 pints vinegar
2 pounds brown sugar
1 teaspoon dry mustard

Wash and prepare each vegetable. Chop and blend. Put vegetables in an enamel pan, sprinkle with salt and let stand overnight. Drain and rinse with clear water. Add vinegar, sugar and mustard and cook gently about one hour. Turn into sterilized jars and seal. Process in boiing water bath for 15 minutes, page 84.

PEAR RELISH

1 peck pears
6 green sweet peppers
6 red peppers
6 large Vidalia onions
1 bunch celery
3 cups sugar
5 cups vinegar
1 Tablespoon salt
1 Tablespoon allspice

Put pears and vegetables through food chopper. Combine sugar, vinegar, salt and allspice; pour into enamel pot with chopped ingredients. Cook about 30 minutes. Put in sterilized jars and seal. Process in boiling water bath, page 84.

SWEET VIDALIA ONION RELISH

4 cups Vidalia onions, chopped
2 cups chopped cabbage
2 cups chopped green peppers
2 cups chopped red peppers
½ cup salt
2 cups white vinegar
2 cups sugar
1 Tablespoon mustard seed
1 Tablespoon celery seed

Wash, clean, and chop the vegetables. Dissolve salt in water; pour over chopped vegetables; let stand overnight (12 hours). Drain; rinse, cover with fresh water; let stand 1 hour; drain. Dissolve sugar in vinegar, add spices; bring to a boil; add drained vegetables and simmmer 15 minutes. Bring to full boil; pack loosely in preheated jars, leaving ¼ inch head space. Fill and close jars. Process for 15 minutes in boiling water bath, page 84. Makes about 3 pints.

VIDALIA ONION-GEORGIA PEACH CHUTNEY

1 large onion, finely chopped
1 cup seedless raisins, chopped
8 pounds peaches, peeled and chopped
2 Tablespoons mustard seed
2 Tablespoons chili powder
1 teaspoon salt
1 teaspoon ground ginger
1 quart vinegar
2¼ cups dark brown sugar
1 garlic clove, minced (optional)

Combine all ingredients in Dutch oven; bring to a boil and simmer uncovered for 1 hour 15 minutes or until mixture is thickened. Pour hot chutney into hot canning jars, leaving ½-inch head space. Remove air bubbles. Wipe jar rims. Adjust lids. Process for 10 minutes in *Boiling Water Bath, page 84. Remove jars from bath and let cool untouched for 12 to 24 hours.

TOMATO SAUCE

1½ cups canned tomatoes
½ cup chopped Vidalia onion
1 sprig parsley
1 bay leaf
2 Tablespoons butter
2 Tablespoons flour.
Salt and pepper

Put the first four ingredients in saucepan and cook gently for 20 minutes; run through a sieve. Press the pulp through the sieve and scrap off all that clings to the under side. Melt butter, add flour and when smooth add the strained tomato, stir until boiling. Season and cook 5 minutes. You may add a teaspoon of sugar to neutralize the acid.

CUCUMBER SAUCE

1 container plain yogurt
1 small grated cucumber
1 Tablespoon fresh dill, chopped
Salt and pepper to taste
1 Tablespoon grated Vidalia onion

Mix all ingredients together. Chill. Stir before serving. Makes 1½ cups.

*BASIC WHITE SAUCE

2 Tablespoons butter
2 Tablespoons flour
1 cup milk
¼ teaspoon salt

Melt butter in saucepan. Stir in flour until smooth. Gradually add milk, stirring constantly. Cook until sauce thickens.

*VIDALIA ONION WHITE SAUCE

2 Tablespoons butter
½ cup chopped onion
2 Tablespoons flour
1 cup milk

Melt butter in skillet. Stir in chopped onion and cook for 5 minutes over medium heat but do not brown. Add flour, mix until smooth. Gradually add milk, stirring constantly. Cook until sauce thickens.

*SPICY SAUCE

⅓ cup steak sauce
¼ cup catsup
¼ cup melted margarine or cooking oil
1 Tablespoon vinegar
1 teaspoon salt
2 Tablespoons grated Vidalia onion (use juice also)

Combine all ingredients and mix well. Makes enough to baste 2 pounds fish fillets.

SOUPS, CHOWDERS AND STEWS

VIDALIA ONION TURKEY SOUP

2 turkey drumsticks
2 quarts water
1 teaspoon salt
2 Vidalia onions, sliced
2 ribs celery, sliced thin
1 bay leaf
1/4 teaspoon thyme
2 cups skim milk
1/2 cup flour
   Fresh parsley for garnish

Cover drumsticks with water. Add salt, onions, celery, bay leaf and thyme. Cook, covered over moderate heat for 1 hour or until tender. Strain broth; let drumsticks cool. Set aside broth until any fat rises to surface. Skim fat. Heat the broth to boiling. Stir milk and flour together. Stir into broth and heat until simmering.

Meanwhile, remove meat from drumsticks and cut into bite size pieces. Discard skin, tendons, and bones. Stir meat into simmering soup until heated through. Garnish with parsley.

PEANUT BUTTER SOUP

1 cup chopped Vidalia onion
2 Tablespoons butter
1 cup peanut butter
3 cups chicken broth
1/4 teaspoon paprika
1 cup light cream or milk

Cook chopped onion in butter about 5 minutes. In large pot add peanut butter, onion, broth and paprika. Boil for 2 minutes. Add cream or milk.

WASTE NOT AN ONION!
Before your Vidalia onions spoil, peel, clean and chop them.
Spread them on a cookie sheet and place in the freezer for one hour.
Put the frozen chopped onions in freezer bags.
Pack them flat in order to break off a portion as needed
for soups, chowders and stews

CREAMY PEACH AND VIDALIA ONION SOUP
"This is nature's goodness made simply elegant"

½ cup finely chopped Vidalia onions
2 Tablespoons butter
1½ Tablespoons flour
   Pinch of salt
1 cup half and half cream
1¼ cups peach puree (canned or fresh peaches)
1 Tablespoon sugar

Melt butter in medium size saucepan; add onion and saute' until tender. Mix in flour and salt and heat until bubbly. (The butter will brown too fast on high heat.) Add the cream, peach puree and sugar. Cook over low to moderate heat, stirring constantly until thick. Serve warm or cold. (A garnish might be a dollop of whipped cream or sour cream.)

This soup can be made a day ahead of time and stored in the refrigerator.

GEORGIA CRACKER SOUP

1 pound dried baby lima beans
3 quarts water
3 slices salt pork or bacon
2 carrots, sliced
1 Vidalia onion, chopped
1 cup chopped celery
   Salt and pepper to taste

Combine beans and water; soak overnight. Drain; add 3 quarts water. Fry salt pork until crisp; add to beans with vegetables and seasonings, cover and simmer for 2 hours. Remove salt pork from soup. Serve with *Lace Cakes, page 39.

VEGETABLE SOUP
"Good Meal In A Bowl"

1½ pounds top round steak, cubed
2 medium Vidalia onions, quartered
¼ cup vegetable oil
2 Tablespoons curry powder
1 package frozen peas, (10 ounces)
1½ teaspoon brown sugar
1½ cups water
1 Tablespoon flour
2 Tablespoons water
2 medium tomatoes, cut into wedges

In large skillet over medium heat, saute' onions in 2 Tablespoons of oil, cook until tender. Remove onions. In remaining oil, cook steak and curry powder until meat loses color. Return onions to skillet; add peas, salt, brown sugar and the 1½ cups water; heat to boiling. Reduce heat, cover, simmer about 8 minutes. Combine flour and 2 tablespoons water; blend well. Add flour mixture to liquid; cook on medium heat until sauce is thickened, stirring constantly. Add tomatoes; cook until heated thoroughly.

VIDALIA ONION-PEANUT VEGETABLE SOUP

¼ cup margarine
½ cup julienne carrots
½ cup julienne zucchini
½ cup julienne green pepper
½ cup shredded red cabbage
½ cup chopped Vidalia onion
3 Tablespoons flour
5 cups chicken broth
1 cup creamy peanut butter
1 cup light cream or milk
½ teaspoon salt
   Roasted peanuts chopped for garnish

In a Dutch oven, melt margarine. Add carrots, zucchini, green pepper, cabbage and onion; saute' about 3 minutes. Add flour and stir until smooth. Gradually stir in chicken broth; bring to a boil. Stir in peanut butter; reduce heat and simmer 15 minutes. Remove from heat. Stir in cream, salt and pepper. Garnish with chopped peanuts if desired. Makes 8 servings.

 Eat a Vidalia onion sandwich with your favorite soup! Put a large slice of onion with bread-and-butter pickles between 2 slices of bread. You will like it!

EGG DROP SOUP

6 cups chicken broth
3 Tablespoons corn starch
½ teaspoon sugar
  Salt and pepper to taste
2 eggs, well beaten
1 cup green spring onions, (chopped with tops)

Heat chicken broth stock in boiling. In small bowl, make a paste of corn starch and ¼ cup cold water or cold broth. Slowly stir corn starch mixture and sugar, salt and pepper into broth. Heat to boiling, stirring constantly. Reduce heat. Add eggs, small amount at a time while stirring to separate them into shreds. Remove from heat. Add onions and stir.

DIETER'S SOUP

1 medium Vidalia onion, chopped
5 chicken bouillon cubes
1 Tablespoon oil (or margarine)
3 medium potatoes, peeled and diced
3 medium carrots, peeled and sliced
½ cup sliced celery
1 Tablespoon chopped parsley
  Salt and pepper to taste
4 cups water

In Dutch oven, saute' onion in oil. Add remaining ingredients. Cover pot, simmer for 30 minutes. Test carrots for doneness.

CHICKEN BROTH FOR SOUPS

1 chicken (3 to 4 pounds)
2 quarts water
2 cups chopped celery
1 Vidalia onion, quartered
1 bay leaf
½ teaspoon parsley flakes
¼ teaspoon thyme leaves
  Dash majoram
  Salt and pepper to taste

Put all ingredients in a Dutch oven and bring to a boil; cover and reduce heat. Simmer for 1 hour. Cool broth, reserve the chicken for salad and use the vegetables in soups.

Chill broth; remove fat that accumulates on the surface. This recipe makes about 8 cups. Put in containers and freeze.

CREAM OF CELERY SOUP

3 ribs celery, cut into 1-inch pieces
1 small Vidalia onion, sliced
3 cups milk
2 Tablespoons butter
2 Tablespoons flour
   Salt and pepper to taste
1 cup cream

Scrub celery and cut into 1-inch pieces. Cook in double boiler over hot water with onion and milk. In large saucepan melt butter; stir in flour, salt, and pepper. Simmer and gradually add celery-milk mixture and cream, stirring until thickened.

VIDALIA ONION VEGETABLE SOUP

1 medium Vidalia onion, chopped
1 Tablespoon margarine
3 medium potatoes, peeled and diced
2 medium carrots, peeled and sliced
1 medium celery stalk, sliced
2 Tablespoons chopped parsley
4 chicken bouillon cubes
   Dash of tarragon
   Salt and pepper to taste
5 cups water

In a heavy Dutch oven, cook onion in margarine. Add remaining ingredients and 5 cups water. Cover and simmer 40 minutes or until vegetables are tender.

POTATO SOUP WITH VIDALIA ONIONS

3 medium potatoes, peeled and diced
1 medium Vidalia onion, minced
2½ cups boiling water
2 Tablespoons butter
2 Tablespoons flour
   Salt and pepper to taste
3 cups milk
2 Tablespoons chopped chives

In large pot, boil potatoes and onion with water. Cover pot and boil 20 to 30 minutes until tender. In a large skillet melt butter. Stir in flour, salt and pepper. Simmer and gradually add milk, stirring until thickened. Add flour mixture to potatoes and onions. Heat thoroughly. Sprinkle chives on top.

 SAVE YOUR VIDALIA ONIONS: Place on cardboard in an air-conditioned room with stem side down. You have to check them often but they will keep several weeks. There must be circulating air.

VEGETABLE CHOWDER

½ cup Vidalia onion and celery, chopped
1 cup carrots, sliced
1 cup potatoes, cubed
1 clove garlic, minced
3½ cups chicken broth
1 can whole kernel corn, drained (17 ounces)
¼ cup margarine
¼ cup unsifted all-purpose flour
2 cups milk
1 Tablespoon prepared mustard
¼ teaspoon pepper and paprika
1 jar chopped pimento, drained (2 ounces)
2 cups shredded Cheddar cheese

Combine first 6 ingredients in a large Dutch oven. Bring to a boil over high heat. Cover; reduce heat and simmer 15 minutes, or until potatoes are tender. Stir in corn, turn off heat. Melt margarine in saucepan over low heat, blend in flour. Add milk; continue cooking, stirring constantly, until thick. Stir in mustard, pepper, paprika, pimento, and cheese. Cook until cheese melts.Pour into vegetable mixture and stir.

SEA-GARDEN CHOWDER

1 pound lean fish fillets, fresh or frozen
½ cup chopped sweet Vidalia onion
2 Tablespoons melted margarine or cooking oil
2 medium potatoes, sliced
1 cup boiling water
¾ teaspoon salt
2 cups milk
1 can cream-style yellow corn (8 ounces)

Thaw fish if frozen. Skin fillets and cut the fillets into pieces about 1 inch square. In a 3 quart saucepan, cook onion in margarine until tender, but not brown. Add the fish, potatoes, water and salt. Cover and simmer for 10 minutes or until fish flakes easily when tested with a fork and potatoes are tender. Add milk and corn; heat but do not boil. Serve hot. Garnish with parsley.

FISH CHOWDER

1 package frozen haddock fillets (1 pound)
1 cup chopped Vidalia onion and celery
1 green pepper, diced coarsely
2 envelopes instant chicken broth mix
1 teaspoon seasoned salt
1 can tomato juice (1 pound can) and 1 cup water

Cut fish into 1 to 2 inch chunks. Combine all ingredients and simmer covered over low heat for 10 minutes. Uncover and simmer about 10 minutes.

SEAFOOD CHOWDER

6 slices salt pork, diced
1 Vidalia onion, chopped
6 potatoes, peeled and diced
2 cups water
1 teaspoon salt
2 pounds cod or haddock, skinned, boned and cut into pieces
1 pound sea scallops, cut in halves
2 boiled lobsters, shelled and cubed
4 cups hot milk
2 cups light cream
¼ cup butter

Cook salt pork until crisp. Add onion, potatoes, water and salt. Simmer covered until almost tender. Add fish, seafood and hot milk. Simmer over low heat for 10 minutes. Add cream and butter. Reheat. Garnish with parsley and paprika.

QUICK AND EASY CLAM CHOWDER

2 slices bacon, diced
1 medium Vidalia onion, finely chopped
1 can condensed cream of potato soup
1 can clams, minced and undrained (6½ ounces)
1 cup heavy cream
¼ cup milk

In a medium saucepan cook bacon and onion until crisp; stir in undiluted soup, clams, cream and milk. Heat slowly, stirring several times, but do not boil. Refrigerate overnight to allow clam flavor to strengthen and reheat without boiling at serving time.

CORN CHOWDER FOR A CROWD

10 slices bacon
4 medium Vidalia onions, chopped
6 medium potatoes, diced
1¾ cans water
4 cans creamed corn
2 cups milk
2 Tablespoons margarine
Salt and pepper to taste

In large Dutch oven fry bacon until crisp. Remove from pan. Pour out fat leaving about 4 tablespoons to saute' onions until soft and tender. Add potatoes and water; cover and cook over medium heat until potatoes are soft, about 15 minutes. Add corn, milk, margarine and seasonings; heat through. Crumble bacon over top and serve with favorite salad and crackers.

HOT-SPICY VIDALIA ONION BEEF STEW

1 pound stew beef
1 can tomatoes, undrained (28 ounces)
½ cup butterbeans, frozen
1 cup carrots and green beans, sliced
½ cup green peas
½ cup corn
¾ cup celery, chopped
1 teaspoon salt
2 large onions, chopped
1 pound okra, sliced
2 medium potatoes, diced
1 can vegetable juice cocktail, (48 ounces)
  Hot sauce to taste
1 Tablespoon Worcestershire sauce
2 teaspoons sugar
½ teaspoon pepper

Combine beef and tomatoes in large Dutch oven. Bring to a boil. Cover; reduce heat and simmer for 1 hour. Add remaining ingredients. Bring to a boil. Reduce heat and simmer, uncovered, until vegetables are tender.

CHICKEN STEW WITH VIDALIA ONIONS

1 whole chicken fryer
1 medium onion, chopped
2 cans tomatoes (16 ounces each)
2 cans creamed corn (16 ounces each)
1 teaspoon seasoned salt

Place chicken and onion in large pot with enough water to cover. Boil unitl tender. Remove chicken, cool, debone and cut into small pieces. Return chicken meat to broth. Add tomatoes, corn and seasoning. Heat thoroughly.

VIDALIA ONIONS IN TURKEY CREOLE

1 Tablespoon butter
1 Vidalia onion, chopped
2 cups turkey, cooked and diced
⅔ cups rice, uncooked
½ cup chopped celery
2 cups turkey broth
1 can tomatoes
  Creole seasonings

In large pot melt butter and saute' onion. Add remaining ingredients cover and cook for 25 minutes.

VIDALIA ONION IN CHICKEN GUMBO

1 large chicken
4 Tablespoons butter
1 large Vidalia onion, chopped
4 quarts water
3 Tablespoons flour
2 Tablespoons butter
1 quart diced okra
¼ cup chopped parsley
2 cans tomatoes
2 cans corn
1 teaspoon sugar
1 can butter beans
   Salt and pepper to taste

Cut up the chicken for frying and fry in boiler in which the gumbo is to be made. Fry until chicken is brown. Remove chicken and saute' onion. Add 4 quarts water, the chicken and cook until meat leaves bones. Remove the boiler from heat. Let chicken cool and remove the bones.

In a saucepan, brown flour in 2 tablespoons butter. Add all vegetables and seasonings, cook for 5 minutes. Then add this mixture to the pot of chicken and cook until vegetables are tender and gumbo is thick.

SHRIMP-OYSTER JAMBALAYA

2 Tablespoons olive oil
2 cups oysters
2 small Vidalia onions, chopped
1 garlic clove, minced
½ cup chopped green pepper
1 pound shrimp, shelled and deveined
1 cup rice, uncooked
1 pound can tomatoes
2 cups chicken broth
1 bay leaf
   Salt and pepper to taste

Heat olive oil in heavy skillet. Add oysters; cook over low heat until edges curl. Remove from skillet and refrigerate. Cook onions, garlic and green pepper in skillet. Add shrimp and cook until pink. Remove from pan. Add rice, tomatoes, broth and seasonings. Cover, simmer until rice is tender and liquid is absorbed. Add oysters and shrimp; heat through.

For a zesty dish with Vidalia onions, melt butter in skillet, add 1 tablespoon honey. When it starts to sizzle, add chopped onions; cook until tender.

 # VEGETABLES

DOUBLED BAKED POTATOES

4 large white potatoes
1 Vidalia onion, chopped
1 stick butter
1/8 teaspoon red pepper
   Salt and pepper to taste
¼ teaspoon black pepper
1 cup sharp cheese, shredded
   Milk

Scrub potatoes, dry and pierce. Bake at 450 degrees F. for about one hour on rack without foil. Melt 2 tablespoons of the butter and saute' onion until clear and tender.

Halve potatoes lengthwise. Scoop out the pulp leaving shells intact. Mash potato pulp; add seasoning, remaining butter, onion and cheese. Put in enough milk for fluffy consistency. Fill shells. Score the tops with a fork. Bake in hot oven until tops are lightly brown.

SPINACH AND TOMATO CASSEROLE

6 green onions, chopped
1 cup chopped Vidalia onion
⅓ cup fine dry bread crumbs
½ teaspoon thyme
   Salt and pepper to taste
   Dash of cayenne
3 eggs, beaten
2 packages frozen chopped spinach, cooked and drained
8 tomato slices
⅓ cup grated Parmesan cheese

Saute' onions in butter in heavy skillet until tender. Combine onions, bread crumbs, pepper, thyme, salt, cayenne, eggs and spinach. Place tomato slices in buttered shallow 3-quart baking dish and top with spinach mixture. Sprinkle with Parmesan cheese. Bake in 350 degree F. oven for 15 minutes.

CREAMED VIDALIA ONIONS

6 medium onions
1 can cream of celery soup
   Cracker crumbs and all-purpose seasoning
2 Tablespoons butter, melted

Peel onions and cook in seasoned water until tender. Put in baking dish; cover with soup, cracker crumbs and butter. Bake in oven at 250 degrees F. until light brown.

CARROT-VIDALIA ONION QUICHE

2 cups carrots, sliced
1 cup water
4 whole cloves and 1 bay leaf
½ cup onion, chopped
1 Tablespoon butter
4 eggs
1 cup milk
½ teaspoon salt
1 cup sharp Cheddar cheese, shredded
1 unbaked 9-inch pie shell

Refrigerate pie shell while preparing filling. Cook carrots in water with bay-leaf and cloves and drain. Saute' onion in butter. Spread on bottom of pie shell. Beat together eggs, milk and salt. Sprinkle half of carrots in pie shell; top with half of cheese. Repeat with remaining carrots and cheese. Pour egg mixture over carrot mixture. Bake for 35 minutes in 375 degree F. oven.

CORN AND CABBAGE STIR-FRY

2 Tablespoons bacon fat or margarine
2 cups chopped cabbage
¼ cup sweet Vidalia onions, chopped
1 cup corn (fresh, frozen or chopped)
   Salt and pepper to taste

Melt fat in heavy skillet over medium heat. Stir- fry cabbage and onion in fat for 3-5 minutes. Add corn to cabbage in skillet. Stir to mix. Cover and cook for 5 minutes. Cabbage should be tender-crisp. Season to taste. Mix lightly and serve.

RICE AND VEGETABLE STIR-FRY

1 cup sliced celery
1 cup thin carrot slices
½ cup green onion slices
½ cup chopped Vidalia onion
1 garlic, minced
¼ cup oil
2 cups hot cooked rice
¼ cup salad dressing
1 Tablespoon soy sauce

Stir-fry celery, carrot, onion and garlic in oil until tender. Add remaining ingredients; stir and cook unitl well heated.

Candied Vidalia Onions: Slice 1 onion and cook with 1 tablespoon butter, brown sugar, peach brandy and amaretto for 5 minutes. Add 1 cup chopped peaches and cook about 2 minutes. Serve with ham.

STUFFED ACORN SQUASH WITH VIDALIA ONIONS

2 medium acorn squash
4 Tablespoons butter or margarine
½ cup chopped Vidalia onion
½ cup chopped celery
⅓ cup chopped bell pepper
½ cup whole wheat bread crumbs
½ teaspoon salt
¼ teaspoon dill
1 cup chopped roasted peanuts
1 cup Cheddar cheese
⅓ cup dark raisins

Cut each squash in half. Scoop out seeds and fiber; discard. Place in a large baking pan. Dot squash halves with 2 tablespoons butter. Bake in 350 degree F. oven for 45 minutes or until soft. Scoop out ⅓ cup squash from each half; set aside.

In heavy skillet, heat 2 tablespoons butter; add onions, celery, bell pepper, saute' 3 minutes. Add bread crumbs, salt, dill, peanuts, cheese, raisins and reserved squash. Mix well. Spoon into squash halves. Return to baking pan; cover with aluminum foil. Bake at 350 degrees F. for 20 minutes, or until heated thoroughly.

FRIED GREEN TOMATOES

4 large green tomatoes
½ cup corn oil
Batter: 2 Tablespoons minced Vidalia onion
¾ cup self-rising flour
½ cup sweet milk
Salt and pepper to taste
Cut firm green tomatoes in ¼ -inch slices.

Make a batter of the onion, flour, milk, salt and pepper. Dip tomatoes into batter. In a thick skillet over medium heat fry tomatoes until brown. Gently turn them and brown the other side. Drain on paper towels and serve while they are hot.

HONEY BAKED VIDALIA ONIONS

6 medium Vidalia onions
1½ cups tomato juice and 1 cup water
2 Tablespoons butter and 3 Tablespoons honey

Peel onions, cut in half and place in buttered dish. Combine remaining ingredients and pour over onions. Bake 45 minutes in 325 degree F. oven.

Before adding the Vidalia onion in dressings and casseroles, sauté in oil or butter.

SKILLET SUPPER SPICED WITH VIDALIAS

3 cups zucchini squash, thinly sliced
1 large Vidalia onion, thinly sliced
1 pound frozen hash brown potatoes
2 Tablespoons chopped chives
⅓ cup butter
½ pound pasteurized process cheese spread
6 cherry tomatoes, halved
4 hard-cooked eggs, sliced
1 cup milk
2 eggs
Salt and pepper to taste

In a large skillet, cook zucchini and onion in small amount of water until tender, about 5 minutes. Drain well and set aside. In skillet over medium heat, melt butter. Add potatoes and chives, cook, turning occasionally for 10 minutes. Stir in zucchini, onion, cheese, cherry tomatoes and 2 of the hard-cooked eggs. Arrange remaining 2 hard-cooked eggs on top. Beat milk, eggs, salt and pepper together. Pour over mixture in skillet. Cover and cook over medium heat until eggs are set, 5 to 10 minutes.

CARROTS AU GRATIN

6 Tablespoons margarine
1½ cups crushed corn flakes cereal
1 cup chopped sweet Vidalia onions
3 Tablespoons all-purpose flour
1 teaspoon salt
Dash of pepper
1½ cups milk
1 cup shredded American cheese
4 cups sliced cooked carrots, drained
1 Tablespoon dried parsley flakes

In heavy skillet, melt 3 tablespoons of margarine and add crushed corn flakes. Set aside for topping. Melt remaining 3 tablespoons margarine in large saucepan over low heat. Add onion. Cook onion until tender but not browned. Stir in flour, salt and pepper. Add milk gradually, stirring until smooth. Increase heat to medium and cook until bubbly and thickened, stirring constantly. Add cheese, stirring until melted. Remove from heat. Stir in carrots and parsley flakes. Spread mixture in buttered glass baking dish, 10x6x2-inches. Sprinkle cereal mixture evenly over top. Bake at 350 degrees F. about 20 minutes or until thoroughly heated. Remove from oven. Let stand about 5 minutes before serving.

Keep cut onions in a closed jar in the refrigerator for several days.

CORN WITH TAMALES AND VIDALIA ONIONS

1 Vidalia onion, chopped
½ cup green pepper, diced
1 jar pimentos (4 ounces)
2 cans creamed corn (1 pound can)
1 can hot tamales (15 ounces)
  Salt and pepper to taste
1 cup shredded sharp cheese

Stew onion, pepper and pimentos in juice from tamales. Add corn, tamales, salt and pepper to sauce mixture. Bake in casserole dish at 350 degrees F. for 1 hour or until mixture thickens. Just before serving, top with grated cheese and return to oven until cheese melts.

HELLY HOT TOMATOES

3 slices bacon
1 cup okra, sliced
1 large sweet Vidalia onion, finely chopped
1 cup celery, chopped
6 tomatoes, finely chopped
1 bell pepper, chopped
  Salt and pepper to taste
2 hot pepper pods
1 pint creamed corn

Fry the bacon and set aside. Seal the edges of okra in the hot bacon fat. Add onions and celery. Saute' until translucent; add chopped tomatoes, bell pepper and hot pepper. Cook all together until tomatoes are well done. Add corn and cook 20 minutes. Before serving crumble the bacon in mixture.

HERBED SPINACH BAKE

2 packages frozen chopped spinach, (10 ounces) cooked and drained
2 cups cooked rice
2 cups shredded process American cheese
4 eggs, beaten
¼ cup melted butter
⅔ cup milk
½ cup chopped Vidalia onion
1 teaspoon Worcestershire sauce
1 teaspoon salt

Combine ingredients; mix well. Use margarine to grease baking dish. Pour mixture in dish. Bake in 350 degrees F. oven for 40 to 45 minutes. Cut into squares.

Fried Vidalias: Spread self-rising flour in a biscuit pan. Dip damp onion rings in the flour; place them on paper towels to dry. Fry them in hot peanut oil to make crisp onion rings.

MARINATED VEGETABLES

2 carrots, cut into sticks
1 cup broccoli flowerets
1 cup cauliflowerets
1 medium cucumber and zucchini, sliced
1 Vidalia onion, sliced and separated into rings
1 cup vegetable oil
½ cup white wine vinegar
1 teaspoon oregano leaves
Salt, pepper and sugar to taste
1 teaspoon dry mustard

Cook carrots in small amount of water in covered saucepan over low heat for 2 minutes. Add broccoli and cauliflower; bring to boiling. Reduce heat; simmer 3 minutes longer. Drain. Combine all vegetables. Combine oil, vinegar, and seasonings; pour over vegetables. Cover and chill at least 8 hours, stirring occasionally.

VIDALIA ONION VEGETABLE MEDLEY

⅓ cup salad oil
3 medium sweet Vidalia onions, sliced
2 cups carrots, sliced
1 cup sliced celery
2 cups shredded cabbage
1 package frozen lima beans (10 ounces)
1 small eggplant, cubed
1 small head cauliflower, broken into flowets
1 green pepper, cut into strips
1 cup chicken stock
Salt and pepper to taste
4 medium tomatoes, cut into wedges

In large kettle cook oil over medium heat. Saute'onions until brown; add remaining ingredients except tomatoes; cook vegetables covered for 20 minutes and stir. Add tomatoes and continue cooking until tomatoes are heated.

OKRA FRITTERS

1 cup chopped Vidalia onion and green tomato
2 cups sliced okra
½ cup chopped green pepper
Salt and pepper to taste
2 eggs, well beaten
½ cup flour and ½ cup corn meal
Vegetable oil

Combine vegetables with seasonings. Add eggs, mixing well. Stir in flour and meal, mixing until moistened. Drop from tablespoon into hot oil in deep fryer. Fry until golden brown.

KRAUT ROUND REUBEN WITH VIDALIA ONIONS

2 cups drained sauerkraut
½ teaspoon caraway or dill seed
  Dash of garlic powder
2 Vidalia onions, sliced
½ cup Russian dressing
1 pound thinly sliced corned beef
1 pound sliced Swiss cheese
  Melted butter
16 slices round bread

Toss kraut with caraway seed and garlic powder; set aside. Spread bread with dressing. Top 8 slices bread with corned beef, onion, kraut, cheese and remaining bread slices.

Brush melted butter on both sides of sandwiches. Grill in skillet until cheese is melted.

POTATO SOUFFLE

3 Tablespoons butter
3 Tablespoons all-purpose flour
1 cup light cream
1 teaspoon sweet Vidalia onion, minced
1 cup mashed potatoes
3 eggs, separated
  Salt and pepper to taste

Melt butter and blend in flour. Add cream and cook, stirring until thickened. Add onion and potatoes. Heat, stirring. Quickly stir in beaten egg yolks. Season. Fold in stiffly beaten egg whites. Pour into 1½ quart souffle dish or casserole. Bake in preheated oven at 350 degrees F. for ½ hour or until puffy and firm.

STEWED OKRA AND TOMATOES

1 small sweet Vidalia onion, chopped
2 slices bacon, cut up
1 small green pepper, chopped (optional)
1 pound okra, cut up
1 pound tomatoes, peeled and chopped
  Salt and pepper to taste

Fry bacon in heavy skillet until brown. Remove and drain. Saute' onion and pepper in bacon fat, add bacon and remaining ingredients; cover and cook 30 to 40 minutes over medium heat.

WATERLESS VIDALIA ONIONS: Use a thick skillet over low heat. Place the sliced onions in the skillet and cover. Cook for 20 minutes, stir often. Use as a vegetable.

SAVANNAH RED RICE

4 slices bacon
1 medium Vidalia onion, chopped
1 cup chopped celery
1 small green pepper, chopped
2 cups uncooked rice
1 can tomatoes, drained and chopped, reserve juice (16 ounces)
1 teaspoon sugar and salt
    Bottled hot pepper sauce to taste
1 can tomato sauce (8 ounces)

Fry bacon until crisp in medium saucepan. Remove form pan. Reserve drippngs. Saute' onion, celery and green pepper in bacon grease until onion is tender. Crumble bacon; return to pan. Add rice; stir to coat with grease. Add tomatoes, sugar, salt and hot sauce. Measure reserved tomato juice and tomato sauce; add water to make 2½ cups liquid. Pour over rice and bring to a boil over high heat, stirring occasionally. Reduce heat, cover and simmer 20 minutes. Remove from heat and let sit covered about 20 minutes. Fluff with a fork.

STUFFED GREEN PEPPERS WITH VIDALIA ONIONS

6 large green peppers, stems and seeds removed
½ pound ground beef, browned
1 cup coarse dry bread crumbs
    Salt and pepper to taste
1 Tablespoon chopped Vidalia onion
1 can tomato soup

Cook peppers in boiling water for 5 minutes; drain. Combine beef, crumbs, seasonings and onion. Add half tomato soup. Stuff peppers with beef mixture; stand upright in small baking dish. Combine remaining soup with ½ soup can of water. Pour over peppers. Bake uncovered for 45 minutes in oven at 325 degrees F. Bake covered for 15 minutes longer..

VERMICELLI WITH BROCCOLI SAUCE

2 Tablespoons minced Vidalia onion
2 Tablespoons margarine
2 Tablespoons all-purpose flour
¼ teaspoon salt
1¾ cups milk
⅓ cup grated Parmesan cheese
1 package frozen, chopped broccoli, cooked and drained (10 ounces)
1 package thin vermicelli, cooked and drained (8 ounces)

Melt margarine in saucepan over low heat. Saute' onion until tender. Blend in flour and salt until smooth; gradually stir in milk. Heat to boiling, stirring constantly. Add cheese; stir until melted. Add broccoli; heat through. Serve over vermicelli.

SCOTCH EGGS WITH CELERY SAUCE
Serve at Ceilidh family party. Come tonight and sing for your supper.

8 hard-cooked eggs
2 pounds bulk sausage meat
1 cup sweet Vidalia onion, grated
1 cup fresh bread crumbs
2 eggs, beaten
1½ cups finely crushed corn flake crumbs
SAUCE:
¼ cup butter or margarine
1 cup celery and leaves, chopped
¼ cup flour
2 cups milk
2 envelopes dehydrated chicken broth
   Salt and pepper to taste

Shell hard-cooked eggs, Place in cold water to cool completely. In a bowl, mix sausage meat, grated onion,(drain off any liquid) bread crumbs, and half of beaten eggs. Remove eggs from cold water. Dry completely so sausage coating will adhere to them. Divide sausage mixture evenly into eight parts and use to encase each hard-cooked egg. Coat sausage meat with other half of beaten eggs, then roll in cornflake crumbs. Chill at least 30 minutes.

Bake coated eggs in preheated 350 degrees F. oven on a shallow greased baking pan. Bake 35 minutes or until brown and crusty.
Sauce: In a medium saucepan, melt butter. Saute' celery and leaves until tender, about 5 minutes. Stir in flour. Cook 30 seconds. Slowly blend in milk. Cook over low heat, stirring constantly, until sauce bubbles. Stir in broth; season to taste. Serve sauce over eggs.

CHEESEY POTATOES IN FOIL

3 large baking potatoes, peeled and sliced
1 large Vidalia onion, sliced
   Salt and pepper
4 slices crisp cooked bacon, crumbled
8 ounces sharp process American cheese, cut in ½ -inch cubes
½ cup butter or margarine, softened

Place potatoes on double thickness of heavy duty foil. Sprinkle with salt, pepper and bacon. Add onion, cheese cubes and dot with butter. Close foil allowing space for expansion of steam; fold edges of foil. With the cover down, cook potatoes on gas grill on low setting for 45 minutes or in conventional oven on 350 degrees F. for 45 minutes.

Place Vidalia onions in pantyhose. Tie a knot between each onion to separate them. **PUT THEM IN THE REFRIGERATOR.** Check them often and remove one when it starts to spoil.

VIDALIA ONION AND GREEN BEAN SALAD

1 pound can green beans, drained
1 pound can mixed vegetables, drained
1 sweet onion, sliced
⅓ cup vinegar
1 pound can sweet peas, drained
1 can chestnuts, drained or roasted peanuts for garnish
¼ cup sugar
2 Tablespoons salad oil
¼ teaspoon pepper
   Salt to taste

In large bowl, combine beans, vegetables, onion and peas. In saucepan, boil vinegar, oil, sugar and seasonings. Pour over the vegetables. Cover and chill several hours, stirring occasionally. Drain vegetables before serving.

SPINACH CHEESE SQUARES AND VIDALIA ONIONS

4 Tablespoons butter
3 eggs, well beaten
1 cup all-purpose flour
1 cup milk
1 teaspoon salt
1 teaspoon baking powder
½ pound sharp cheese, grated
1 medium onion, grated
2 packages frozen chopped spinach, drained

Melt butter in 9 x 13 x 2-inch baking pan in the oven. Remove from oven. In large mixing bowl combine eggs, flour, milk, salt and baking powder, mix well. Add grated cheese, onion and drained spinach. Pour into pan and bake for 35 minutes at 325 degrees F. Cool thoroughly and cut into squares.

FRESH SPINACH PIQUANT

6 slices bacon, chopped
1 medium Vidalia onion, sliced
2 pounds fresh spinach
½ teaspoon oregano leaves
1 Tablespoon vinegar
   Salt and pepper

In skillet, fry bacon. Drain off fat leaving about 2 tablespoons. Saute' onion rings until tender. Remove from fat. Wash, cut up spinach and add to fat. Add oregano; cover and cook 10 minutes. Add vinegar, salt, pepper, onion rings and bacon. Toss lightly. *"You will enjoy one of your daily food requirements."*

 A wet Vidalia onion is easier to peel than a dry one.

SWEET VIDALIA ONION GRITS

8 slices bacon
1 medium sweet onion, chopped
2 Tablespoons green pepper, finely chopped
1 can tomatoes, chopped
½ teaspoon sugar and salt
6 cups water
1½ cups uncooked regular grits

In skillet, fry bacon until crisp. Drain; crumble and set aside. Pour off grease; use 2 tablespoons to saute' onion and pepper.Stir in tomatoes and sugar. Bring to a boil; reduce heat and simmer 30 minutes.

In large pot, bring water and salt to a boil; stir in grits slowly to keep from lumping. Cook 20 minutes, stirring until grits are thickened. (The more you stir, the better the taste.) Spoon into serving dish; pour vegetable mixture on top and sprinkle with bacon.

BROCCOLI CASSEROLE

2 packages frozen chopped broccoli (10 ounces each)
1 can cream of mushroom soup
1 cup mayonnaise
1 cup roasted peanuts, chopped
2 eggs, beaten
1 medium Sweet Vidalia onion, chopped
¼ cup butter or margarine, melted
2 cups dry bread crumbs
1 cup grated sharp Cheddar cheese

Cook broccoli with salt according to package directions; drain. Add soup, mayonnaise, peanuts, eggs and onion, mix well. Pour broccoli mixture into greased 2 quart casserole dish. Sprinkle with grated cheese and top with buttered bread crumbs. Bake at 350 degrees F. for 30 minutes.

SWEET POTATOES WITH VIDALIAS AND PORK

5 medium sweet potatoes, cooked and sliced
1 large Vidalia onion, sliced thin
   Pork Roast, cooked and sliced and chopped
1 cup milk

Butter a large baking dish. Place a layer of potatoes in the bottom, a layer of onion slices, a layer of pork slices and continue layers until dish is full. Pour milk over layers and bake for 30 minutes in 350 degrees F. oven.

CABBAGE CASSEROLE

2 medium Vidalia onions, sliced
1 medium size cabbage, cut in small sections
1 can cream of mushroom or celery soup
½ cup mayonnaise
   Crumbled crackers (any kind)
1 cup grated cheese

Boil onions in small amount of water until tender. Steam cabbage in water until tender, about 10 minutes. Drain. Mix the cabbage with the onions and onion water. Mix mushroom or celery soup and mayonnaise and stir well. In a casserole dish, place a layer of cracker crumbs, cabbage mixture, one half of soup mixture. Repeat with remainder of ingredients. Bake in 350 degrees F. oven for 30 minutes. Top with grated cheese. Put in oven for 10 minutes or until cheese melts.

BARLEY PILAF WITH PEAS

3 cups water
3 chicken bouillon cubes
1 cup Quick Pearled barley
1 package frozen peas (10 ounces)
½ cup chopped Vidalia onion
1 clove garlic, minced
2 Tablespoons margarine
   Crispy cooked bacon for garnish

Bring water and bouillon cubes to boil; stir in barley. Reduce heat; cover. Simmer 10 minutes or until tender, stirring occasionally; drain. In large skillet, saute' frozen peas, onion and garlic in margarine; reduce heat. Stir in cooked barley, continue cooking until heated through. Garnish with crisp bacon.

POTATO CASSEROLE WITH VIDALIA ONIONS

8 medium potatoes
   Salt and pepper to taste
1 package of cream cheese (8 ounces)
2 eggs, beaten
2 Tablespoons all-purpose flour
2 Tablespoons dry minced parsley
2 Tablespoons sweet onion, grated
1 can French fried onion rings (3½ ounces)

Cook potatoes and mash. Add salt and pepper, cream cheese and beat. Add eggs, flour, parsley and onion; mix well. Put in buttered dish. Sprinkle onion rings on top of mixture and bake uncovered at 325 degrees F. about 30 minutes.

Enjoy Vidalia onions in several colors. The recipe *Colorful Vidalia Onions is on page 65. Use them in decorations and vegetables.

COOKING IN GEORGIA

GEORGIA SWEET POTATO PIE

2 eggs
2 cups sweet potatoes, cooked and mashed
1 cup sugar
½ stick butter, melted
¾ cup evaporated milk
½ teaspoon nutmeg
½ teaspoon cinnamon
¼ teaspoon allspice

Beat the eggs, add all other ingredients. Pour into an unbaked pie shell. Bake at 350 degrees F. for 45 minutes.

PECAN PIE

½ cup sugar
1 cup white corn syrup
4 Tablespoons butter
1 Tablespoon vanilla
1 cup pecans, whole or chopped
3 eggs, beaten

Combine sugar, syrup; add eggs, butter, vanilla and nuts. Mix well and pour into uncooked pastry. Bake for 10 minutes at 400 degrees F. Lower temperature to 300 degrees F. and cook 35 minutes.

CRACKLIN' BREAD

1½ cups stone-ground meal
½ cup all-purpose flour
2 teaspoons baking powder
1 teaspoon sugar
½ teaspoon salt
½ teaspoon soda
1 cup cracklins, chopped fine
1½ cups buttermilk
2 eggs, beaten

Sift dry ingredients together. Combine milk, eggs and cracklins. Mix together. Pour into a well greased iron skillet. Bake in hot oven at 400 degrees F. for 25 minutes or until golden brown.

WATERMELON SHERBERT

10 cups ripe watermelon
¼ cup lemon juice
1 cup sugar

Put watermelon in blender with sugar and puree. Add lemon juice. Pour in bowl and stir until sugar dissolves. Freeze in ice cream churn as directed for sherbert.

PEANUT BRITTLE

2 cups granulated sugar
1 cup light corn syrup
½ cup water
½ teaspoon salt
3 cups raw shelled peanuts, skins on
2 Tablespoon butter
2 teaspoon baking soda

Heat sugar, syrup, water and salt to a rolling boil in a heavy saucepan. Add peanuts. Reduce heat to medium and stir constantly. Cook until syrup spins a thread. Add butter, then baking soda. Beat rapidly and pour on a buttered surface spreading to ¼-inch thickness. When cool break into pieces. Store in an airtight container. Yields about 2 pounds.

Microwave Oven Method:

1½ cups raw shelled peanuts, skins on
1 cup granulated sugar
½ cup light corn syrup
1/8 tsp. salt
1 teaspoon butter
1 teaspoon vanilla
1 teaspoon baking soda

Stir together peanuts, sugar, syrup, and salt in a 1½ quart microwave safe container. Cook 8 minutes on high in microwave oven stirring well after 4 minutes. Stir in butter and vanilla. Microwave 2 minutes longer on high. Add baking soda and quickly stir until light and foamy. Immediately pour onto lightly greased baking sheet; spread to ¼-inch thickness. When cool break into pieces. Store in airtight container.

SUGAR-COATED PEANUTS

1 cup granulated sugar
½ cup water
2 cups raw shelled peanuts, skins on

Dissolve sugar in water in saucepan on medium heat. Add peanuts and continue to cook over medium heat, stirring frequently. Cook until peanuts are completely sugared. (Coated and no syrup). Pour on ungreased cookie sheet, separate peanuts with a fork. Bake at 300 degrees for 20-30 minutes, stirring every 10 minutes.

CAMP STEW

1 chicken, big fryer or hen
3 or 4 medium potatoes, diced
3 or 4 Vidalia onions, diced
Fresh or canned tomatoes
Seasoned salt

Cook chicken until it falls off bone. Cool and debone it. Cut into small pieces. Remove grease from the top of liquid. Add onions, potatoes, and crushed tomatoes. Simmer several hours.

Camp stew should be the consistency of Brunswick stew. Add water as needed. This recipe can be prepared the day before your campers arrive.

PEACH POUND CAKE

1 cup butter, softened
3 cups sugar
6 eggs
3¾ cups sifted all-purpose flour
½ teaspoon baking powder
1 cup milk
1 teaspoon almond extract
1 package fresh frozen peaches, thawed and diced (16 ounces)

Cream butter and sugar until light and fluffy. Add eggs, one at a time, beating well after each addition. Sift together flour and baking powder. Add to creamed mixture alternately with milk, beginning and ending with flour mixture. Add almond extract. Stir in peaches; mix well. Pour into greased and floured 10-inch tube pan. Preheat oven to 350 degrees F. Bake 1 hour 30 minutes. Cool 15 minutes before removing from pan.

GEORGIA PEACH COBBLER

1 stick butter
1 cup sugar
1 cup self-rising flour
¾ cup milk
1 quart fresh peaches or 1 large can sliced peaches, undrained

Preheat oven to 350 degrees F. Melt butter in baking dish. Combine flour, milk and sugar, pour in dish. Pour peaches and juice on top. **DO NOT STIR.** Bake for 45 minutes. The batter will cook up through the fruit and form a crust. If you want juicy cobbler, double the milk. For sweeter cobbler, add more sugar. This is good served with vanilla ice cream.

AUNT CLARA'S WINE

1 quart grapes
1 yeast cake
5 cups of sugar
1 quart water

Mash grapes. Mix the sugar with the quart of water until dissolved; add yeast cake, grapes and mix well. Pour into a gallon glass jar. Finish filling it with water. Tie a muslin cloth with a cord around the top of the jar. Let it stand for 28 days in a cool room. Strain wine into bottles. Cap bottles with cork screws.

MINT JULEPS

1 cup sugar
1 bunch fresh mint sprigs, about 2 cups lightly packed
1 cup water
Crushed ice
Bourbon

Combine sugar, water and boil for 5 minutes without stirring. Cool. Place mint in a jar and pour syrup over it. Seal with lid. Refrigerate overnight. Remove mint. Keep syrup refrigerated. This will keep several weeks and individual juleps may be made as desired.

For each serving: Fill an 8-ounce glass with crushed ice. Add 1 tablespoon syrup, 1 tablespoon water and 2 ounces bourbon. Stir until glass is frosted; garnish with a sprig of mint.

SWEET POTATO BALLS

3 cups mashed sweet potatoes
3 Tablespoons butter, melted
½ cup sugar
½ cup pecans, chopped
Corn flakes, crushed
½ teaspoon salt
½ teaspoon maple flavoring
1 egg, beaten
Large marshmallows
Coconut

Add potatoes, salt, butter, sugar, egg, maple flavoring and pecans. Mix well and mold into a ball around a marshmallow. Roll in crushed corn flakes or coconut. Place on an oiled baking pan and bake at 350 degrees F. until hot and slightly browned.

COOKING SUGGESTIONS

1. A wet Vidalia onion is easier to peel than a dry one.

2. To peel a large quantity of onions, cover them with hot water for 3 to 5 minutes and the skins will come off easily.

3. Before adding the Vidalia onion in dressing, stuffings and casseroles, saute' the onion in oil or butter.

4. If you need the juice of an onion, squeeze half an onion with the skin on it. Use a lemon squeezer.

5. Keep cut onions in a closed glass jar in the refrigerator for several days.

6. When you need a small portion of an onion, do not peel the whole onion. Cut the size needed and peel it. The larger portion will keep longer with the skin on it in the refrigerator.

7. If you want an onion as mild as possible, cut the onion into rings and soak them in cool water for 1 hour or in 2 cups of warm water with 1 teaspoon of sugar for 1 hour.

8. Before your Vidalia onions spoil, peel and boil them until soft but not mushy. Chop them in a blender; pour into plastic bags and freeze. Use them for soups, sauces and stews.

NUTRITIONAL VALUE OF THE ONION

Nutritionally, onions are low in calories and provide the diet with Vitamin C, the B-vitamins and several minerals. The chart below gives the nutritional content of 100 grams on onions (about ¾ cup of chopped onions). This information is taken from the U.S.D.A. handbook, No. 8, Table 1.

Calories 38
Protein . . . . 1.2 grams
Fat . . . . 0.1 grams
Carbohydrates . . . . 8.7 grams
Ash . . . . 0.6 grams
Calcium . . . . 27 milligrams
Phosphorus . . . . 36 milligrams
Iron . . . . 0.5 milligrams
Sodium . . . . 10 milligrams
Potassium . . . . 157 milligrams
Vitamin A . . . . trace (yellow onions, 40)
Thiamine . . . . 03 milligrams
Riboflavin . . . . 04 milligrams
Niacin . . . . 2 milligrams
Vitamin C . . . . 10 milligrams

118

RECIPES